S0-BJZ-017

The Online Classroom

Teaching with the Internet

Fourth Edition

by Eileen Giuffré Cotton

ERIC Clearinghouse on Reading, English, and Communication

EDINFO Press

Published 2000 by
ERIC Clearinghouse on Reading, English, and Communication
Carl B. Smith, Director
2805 East 10th Street, Suite 150
Bloomington, Indiana 47408-2698

and

EDINFO Press
P.O. Box 5247
Bloomington, Indiana 47407

Editor: James Opiat
Book Design and Production: David J. Smith
Cover Design: Inari Information Services, Inc.

Copyright © 2000 by EDINFO Press
All rights reserved.
Printed in the United States of America

ERIC (an acronymn for Educational Resources Information Center) is a national network of sixteen clearinghouses, each of which is responsible for building the ERIC database by identifying and abstracting educational resources, including research reports, curriculum guides, conference papers, journal articles, and government reports. The Clearinghouse on Reading, English, and Communication (ERIC/REC) collects educational information specifically related to reading, English, journalism, speech, and theater at all levels. ERIC/REC also covers interdisciplinary areas, such as media studies, reading and writing technology, mass communication, language arts, critical thinking, literature, and many aspects of literacy.

This publication was prepared with partial funding from the Office of Educational Research and Improvement, U.S. Department of Education, under contract no. RR93002011. Contracts undertaking such projects under government sponsorship are encouraged to express freely their judgement in professional and technical matters. Points of view, however, do not necessarily represent the official view or opinions of the Office of Educational Research and Improvement.

Dedication

To Chet, my best friend and my husband. Thank you for keeping me calm, cool, and collected.

ERIC/REC Advisory Board

Elaine Aoki
Bush School
Seattle, Washington

Douglas Barnard
Mesa Public Schools
Mesa, Arizona

Neyland Clark
Cape Girardeau School District #63
Cape Girardeau, Missouri

James Gaudino
National Communication Association
Annandale, Virginia

Earlene Holland
Office of Program Development
Indianapolis, Indiana

Joan Irwin
International Reading Association
Newark, Delaware

Robert Pavlik
Cardinal Stritch University
Milwaukee, Wisconsin

Lenore Sandel
ASCD Whole Language Newsletter
Rockville Center, New York

Faith Schullstrom
National Council of Teachers of English
Urbana, Illinois

Josefina Tinajero
Mother and Daughter Program
El Paso, Texas

The Online Classroom: Teaching with the Internet

by Eileen Giuffré Cotton

Fourth Edition

Table of Contents

Section 1: Learning

Section 2: Lessons

Acknowledgments

A book is the work of many people, not just the author. Specifically, I want to thank all the K–12 teachers who gave me ideas for lessons, the folks at ERIC/REC for their time, energy and patience, and my friends and colleagues for all the encouragement they gave me. Thank you, one and all.

About the Author

Eileen Giuffré Cotton is a worldwide teacher. She has taught in public schools in California, at the University of Guam and now as a Professor of Education at California State University, Chico where she teaches Reading. Her travels have taken her to every state in the U.S. and all but one province and territory in Canada, the British Isles, the Orient, and Down Under. Her summers are spent in Wyoming with Chet (her husband of 28 years) on their mountainside, where she wrote *The Online Classroom*. She collects teddy bears, drives a diesel pickup truck, likes RVs and steam engines, and recently bought her ninth computer. She divides her time between The Star Valley in Wyoming and The Big Valley in California.

CHAPTER	GRADES			
	K–3	4–6	7–8	9–12
1: The World Wide Web		n/a		
2: A Wealth of Web Sites		b	b	b
3: Searching on the Web—Directories and Search Engines		b	b	b
4: Developing and Designing a Web Site		b	b	b
5: Using the Internet for Teaching—Rules for the Road		n/a		
6: The Past, Present, and Future of the Web		n/a		
7: E-pals and Keypals	e	e	e	e
8: A Whale of a Time!		b	b	
9: The CyberNews		b	b	b
10: The ABCs of Canada		b	b	
11: Virtually Together in D.C.		b	b	b
12: Get a Job!				b
13: A Book an Hour			b	b
14: The Ambassador to Mexico WebQuest			b	b
15: The Games People Play	b	b	b	b
16: Just for the Little Kids	b			

e: E-mail   b: Web browser   n/a: not applicable

This matrix indicates the appropriate grade level(s) and required technology for the activities described in each chapter.

The Basics

The first time I was online was in 1976, with a free e-mail account from the university I was attending. It was fun, but very limiting, as there were not too many people online 20+ years ago. For the next several years, I tried to get online at my university, but to no avail. Then I saw an advertisement for ten free hours from America Online. I sent away for the program. As soon as I got it, I loaded it in my computer, set up my modem, and away I went. It was fun, but then I like to push buttons and play

with gadgets and toys, so connecting to AOL was a logical extension of a natural bent. I started to play with the different departments available, and I soon ran out of free time. There was so much to do, and so little time to do it! The next fall, my university provided all faculty members with an e-mail account, and computer access to the Internet via Mosaic, Turbo Gopher, Fetch, and Telnet. Being the pro who had already played with AOL, I figured I knew what all this good stuff was about, so I set out to explore some more. I did not then know that my university offered so many more services than AOL, even though AOL had a prettier set of graphics. I've been using either my university server, or a local service provider ever since.

I visited hundreds of sites, and decided the Internet was a lot of fun and held great potential for my students, until I ran out of time again. Then came Winter Break. I spent 3,000 minutes on the Internet, exploring, learning, crashing into virtual walls, surviving the crashes, and becoming convinced this was not only a place to learn and have a good time, but also another way to teach my students.

The learning I was doing was fascinating and interesting. My perseverance paid off, and soon I wanted more out of the Net. I wanted to set up Web pages and develop lists and links and lessons for future explorations and learning. I wanted to get my students connected to the Internet, so they could explore the usefulness of this tool. In a nutshell, all the surfing and crashing I did led eventually to this book.

Organization of *The Online Classroom*

This book has two sections: *Learning*, and *Lessons*. The first section deals with the programs you will need to use the Internet, as well as several hundred great Web sites for teachers, how to manage the Internet classroom, and how to search the Internet effectively and easily. The second section contains lessons with clearly stated goals, rationales, objectives, procedures and evaluation guidelines. Chapter 6 is a new addition to the fourth edition. It provides some help in assessing the Internet-ability of your class, and how to design lessons in general. Throughout the book, there are changes from the last edition, mainly from ideas I have gleaned from working with teachers all over the World. I hope you find them useful.

Unlike many books about the Internet, this book starts out with the easiest things to do, and progresses from there. As the book proceeds—and you become more confident—the chapters become more challenging. In addition, because I want you to feel comfortable using the Internet, I encourage you to have lots of practice using the relevant software before your students access it.

When you feel confident about using the Internet, you will be better able to teach with it. To make the lessons more accessible, all the URLs (Uniform Resource Locators or "links") you'll need are written for you. They are also located at the Web site for *The Online Classroom* at **http://www.csuchico.edu/Online_Classroom**, where you can click on them directly. As you look at the lesson plans, you will see that some can be finished in a single day, while others are units of instruction that will take from two to five weeks (or more) to complete. You can use this book to integrate use of the Internet into your entire classroom curriculum. Once you have grasped the basics of how the Internet can serve you as a teacher, you will be "walking the Web" to explore your own questions and interests. You will discover a wealth of information out there that you never imagined was so readily available. You may reinvent your entire approach to teaching and learning. All of that is up to you.

You will notice that I have not stated exact grade levels for the lessons. I've been using computers and the Internet with elementary, middle school, and high school students, so each lesson is designed to adapt easily to your specific classroom situation. You can make each lesson either easier or more difficult, depending on the grade level and ability of your students. When students are learning something new, they do not seem to mind material that might appear too simple. However, once they have learned a particular Internet process or technique, most students are able to find their appropriate levels of use and engagement.

All of the lessons encourage small-group work and cooperative learning. Sitting in front of a computer by oneself can be lonely. Working with someone else is more interesting and fun, and it doubles your thinking and creative power, as well as your ability to troubleshoot and solve problems. The Internet itself is based upon connections between ideas, and when two or three students work together at an Internet-connected computer, the potential for connectivity increases exponentially. These pages, therefore, do not contain quiet-corner lessons that will not disrupt a classroom full of students. These lessons will stir up the noise of learning, and provoke talk and laughter. This is good. Your job is to encourage the positive noise and discourage the negative, while monitoring the process to ensure that your students are walking the Web safely and staying on task. In addition, if you share the experience of learning how to use the Internet with a fellow teacher, you will enjoy both the book and the Internet a whole lot more.

Time

"All of this sounds great," you are probably thinking to yourself right now. *The Online Classroom* has directions for using the most popular software needed to access the Internet; it has lessons you can use right away; it has its very own Web site at **http://www.csuchico.edu/Online_Classroom**; and it is associated with a three credit-hour, graduate-level class at Indiana University, that you can register for now. Just visit the IU distance education page at **http://education.indiana.edu/~disted/530ol.html**. So, what's the problem? The problem is *time*. The Internet, like a huge shopping mall, is sometimes hard to leave. There is so much information out there and you want to see it all. Finding out new information that is of interest to you and your students, checking out the latest, up-to-the-minute news, and making connections with people and ideas half a world away, are very addictive pastimes. I have not yet solved this problem for myself, so I have little advice to offer!

Are you ready?

By now, I hope I've whetted your appetite, and you are eager to get started "walking the Web" and sharing the wealth of the Internet with your students. There is a lot more to learn, but the best way to learn is to *do*. Are you ready to put on your Web-walking shoes? Let's start walking the Web of information!

Please write to me at **cotton@instruction.com**. I love to hear from teachers who tell me what they are doing in their classes.

Section 1
Learning

Chapter 1
The World Wide Web

The single most amazing event in the last ten years has been the spread of the Internet. Since the Internet started in 1969 with a few select users worldwide, it has grown and blossomed into a way of life for many people. Today, people in just about every country in the world have Internet access. When every television program has a Web presence and most of your friends have a Web page and an e-mail address, it is probably correct to say that the Web is here to stay. This is a far cry from when I wrote the first edition of this book in 1995. No one thought "it" would last this long. Little did they know!

You may have been working on the Internet for a time, but do you know how it works? I'll try not to be too technical, but feel free to skip over the next couple of paragraphs if you are not interested in how the Internet connects us all together. The Internet is a worldwide network of computers, primarily connected through ordinary phone lines. Some computers connected to the Internet are called *servers*, and they store information that can be retrieved from other computers that are called *clients*. When you use your computer to retrieve or download information from the Internet, your computer is a client getting information from a server.

The World Wide Web consists of connected servers and clients, that communicate using a common set of communication proto-

cols. Using the same protocols allows different kinds of computers—from a million-dollar mainframe to a used PC—to communicate with each other. (Think of protocols as manners, like you use
at a large family gathering—rules for how to leave the room
politely, how to greet someone, etc.) These protocols allow your
computer (the client) to retrieve text, pictures, sounds, and other
types of files from any other computer (the server), via the
Internet. However, to retrieve that information, you need a
program on your computer that understands these protocols: a
Web browser.

There are many Web browsers out there. You might hear of
programs such as Cello, Mosaic, Lynx, and MacWeb, but the two
preeminent Web browsers are Netscape Navigator and Microsoft
Internet Explorer. All Web browsers do the same thing: Allow you
to read, hear and experience pages on the World Wide Web; send
and receive e-mail; read newsgroups, etc. (where etc. is even a bit
more than you expect). Some browsers let you read only the text;
while others let you read text, view graphics, hear music, and
experience vivid animation. Netscape and Internet Explorer allow
you to do all of the latter. That's what makes them so popular!
Most people use either Netscape *or* Internet Explorer. I use both.
When I'm on my Macintosh, I use Netscape; when I'm on my PC, I
use Explorer. As far as I'm concerned, they're equivalent.

Netscape Navigator/Communicator and Microsoft Internet
Explorer are the two best browsers available right now. Both
companies are trying to develop the best browser, in order to have
the largest share of the market. Both browsers do exactly the
same thing and which one is the best really depends on the user.
Tomorrow or next week, someone else will develop a better
browser, with faster download times, more built-in multimedia,
and bells and whistles I cannot even imagine. The Internet, and
ways to navigate it, are changing every day. To be a successful
Web-walker, you need to be flexible. If you're not flexible, you can
easily become tangled in a spider Web of information!

If you want to upgrade to a newer, faster browser, go to Netscape
(**http://home.netscape.com/download/index.html**) or Microsoft
(**http://www.microsoft.com/msdownload/iebuild/msnie5/en/
msn.asp**) and download the browser of your choice for free. Once
at either site, you will need to indicate the type of computer, and/
or operating system you have (Macintosh, Windows95/NT/98,

DOS, UNIX), click on the correct link, and wait while it downloads. These programs are easy to download, but because of their size it may be a time-consuming process. Depending on the speed of your Internet connection, it may take two hours or more. Don't be discouraged! If you have a newer computer, then one or both of these browser programs will already be part of the software that came with your computer. Also, when you subscribe to an Internet Service Provider (ISP), that service should either provide you with a browser program of your choice, or at least show you how to download it from the Web.

Netscape Navigator

To work with any browser, you need to know some technical vocabulary. All the words I'll be using are in the glossary at the end of the book, so if you come across something that is confusing, look back there for a friendly definition. Please note: if you are using Microsoft Internet Explorer you can skip to page 16.

Look at the picture of the Netscape Navigator screen below, and let's play with the menus and buttons to find out what they can

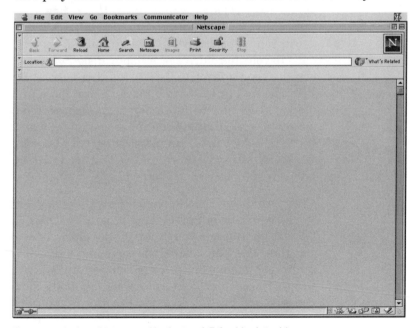

Browser window (Netscape Navigator 4.5 for Macintosh)

do. If you have Netscape loaded on your computer, it might be easier to work with both your computer window and the pictures in the book. If your computer and your browser are different from mine don't worry. As you will see, they are similar enough. Each browser looks slightly different on each platform version (Macintosh, Windows, UNIX, etc.), so be patient, be flexible, and try to translate what I am saying into what you see on the screen. Both Netscape and Internet Explorer rely on these buttons and pull-down menus as the easy-to-operate controls of the program. You need not memorize them—it will come with practice.

Pull-Down Menus

The top row displays the title of the Web page you are currently viewing. Immediately below that is a row of pull-down menus: File, Edit, View, Go, Communicator, and Help.

Click on File, then click on Open Page. Open Page provides a window for you to type in a URL (Web address). After typing, click on OK, and your browser will take you to that address. Open Page will open an HTML file from your hard drive or a diskette, as opposed to an Internet file. Open Page is used a lot when you are creating HTML documents, as this is how you check them for accuracy. (I'll explain this in more detail in Chapter 4.) Further down, you will see Save As, where you can save the text of a Web page to your hard drive or a floppy disk; Send Page, in case you want to send a favorite URL to another person; Print Preview and Print, as well as Quit (on a Mac), or Exit (on a PC). You should always know how to quit a program! Also located under File is the option to work offline. Sometimes you might want to use your browser, but do not want to be connected to the Internet. Click on Work Offline, and you will not be bothered with your computer trying to dial up your server.

Click on Edit and see the usual Cut, Copy, and Paste commands found on most word processing programs. There is also a Select All option, that lets you group all the pieces of a whole Web page together. The Edit commands come in handy when you are using a browser and a word processing program, since they allow you to use all the normal word processing functions, such as blocking, copying, and pasting from the browser to the word processing program. The last item on the Edit menu is Preferences. This is

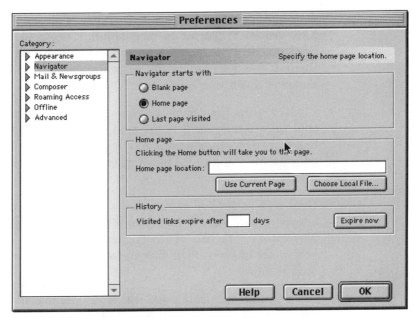

Preferences window (Netscape Navigator 4.5 for Macintosh)

important. Study it carefully. Set your preferences to suit your needs. Click on Preferences and a window pops up. This window lets you control your Web identity, the appearance of your screen, clear the cache, and more.

Click on Appearance, and you can change the size of the display font. Click on Navigator, and you can change your home page to any page you want it to be. I set my husband's browser to show my picture every time he starts up, so he won't forgot who I am. If you are learning how to use the Internet, I suggest you start out with the home page for this book: **http://www.csuchico.edu/ online_classroom**. That way, you can read the chapters and click on the appropriate URLs at the same time.

Click on Mail & Newsgroups, and write in your e-mail address and identity. Click on Advanced, and Allow Cookie Access. (A cookie is a small amount of information that the Web site leaves on your hard drive, so you can be identified for future reference. Some people like to turn off cookies, some don't. I leave cookies on.) Lastly, click on the + sign in front of advanced, and another string of words appear. Click on Cache, which is a storage area on your hard drive. In the cache are copies of all the Web pages you have visited. When the cache gets full, it needs to be emptied. Click on Clear Memory Cache and Clear Disk Cache to empty them. If you don't empty the cache regularly, it will become full and slow down your computer.

Click on View, then Show, to turn off and on the three toolbars that we will talk about in the next section. Click on Page Source, to see the HTML code for a Web page source code. This is a very educational thing to do. In Chapter 4 you will learn more about HTML.

Click on Go, and you are greeted with a list of the most recent sites you have visited during your current Web-walking session. Now click on the title of any document, Web page, or link to which you would like to return directly (as opposed to going Back one step at a time).

Click on Communicator, and this leads you to some of the other properties of Netscape. Click on Messenger, and the e-mail program appears. Click on Composer, and you have the built-in HTML program. Click on Conference, and you can set up an Internet conference call, using either your voice (if you have a microphone) or your keyboard, to "talk" to another person. Click on AOL Instant Messenger and you will see if your e-mail friends are online right now. Point to Tools and a side menu rolls out. Click on History to see all the Web sites your computer has visited. If you forget a URL, you can search History to find it. You can also clear History by going back to Preferences in the Edit menu. Click on Navigator, then the button marked Clear History.

Click on Help, and you can find information about all the menus, buttons, and features in the program. I know it's not "cool" to read help manuals, but if you don't tell anyone, I won't tell on you.

Toolbars

There are three rows of toolbars on Netscape: Navigation Toolbar, Location Toolbar, and Personal Toolbar. Remember, in the View menu you can show or hide any of these toolbars. For personal use, I like all of them; for school use I hide the personal toolbar.

Navigation, Location, and Personal toolbars (Netscape Navigator 4.5 for Macintosh)

The Navigation Toolbar

The Navigation Toolbar buttons let you navigate more easily around the Web and have many of the same functions as the pull-down menus. The first button is Back. If the Back button is dimmed, then it is not yet activated—since you have not gone anywhere yet, there's no "back" for Back to go to. As you walk the Web, Back will darken, then you can click on Back to go back to wherever you were before, one step at a time, until you finally arrive where you started. To speed up the process, use Go in the pull-down menus.

Click on Forward, and it takes you forward along the path you have been traveling. This way you can move back and forth, revisiting sites without losing your way or having to re-key long URL addresses.

Click on Reload to update a Web page, or when pages don't come through completely. Reload will give you the newest version of the page you are looking at. This is especially important when you are visiting a site that changes frequently. At some Web sites you can click on Reload every few minutes to reveal a new picture of the weather outside or the latest stock market information.

Click on Home, and you will automatically return to the home page that you designated in Preferences. Netscape has this page preset to their own NetCenter, but there is no reason why you cannot change it to any page on the Web. For school, change the home page button to a favorite search tool or to the main Web page of a lesson you are teaching.

Search will take you to the Netscape NetCenter search page. When you click on this button you will see a screen that will let you search the Web. You can also choose one of several search tools, such as Excite, Infoseek, Lycos, Snap, LookSmart, Directory, and others as your default search tool.

My Netscape allows you to personalize Netscape to meet your needs. Here you can create your personal start page. Click on My Netscape and you will be given directions for customizing this page to include information that Netscape thinks is important to you. I consider this an advertising gimmick, as it will lead you to Netscape NetCenter one more time.

By clicking the Print button, you can print out the Web page that is on your screen. If you have a color printer, the page will be printed in the colors that you see on the screen. The next button is Security. The icon is a padlock. If the padlock is open, then the page is not secure, meaning the text is not encrypted or coded. Other people can read your information if they know how. If the padlock is closed, then the page is secure. Notice the padlock when you click on a page. If you are going to be transferring information that is personal, such as credit card numbers or social security numbers, over the Web, make sure you are on a secure Web site with the padlock in the locked position.

Stop can be one of the most useful buttons around. Sometimes your browser will grind and grind, and will grind forever, trying to load a document. Click on Stop, and about eighty percent of the time it will stop! Then, when you start over, the page may load like a charm (and they call this scientific!). Stop is a great time-saver, one that I use a lot. Most browsers have a Stop function. Thank goodness, since waiting is something that I am not good at doing!

The Location Toolbar

Just below the Navigation toolbar is the Location toolbar. It includes Bookmarks, Go To, and What's Related. Click on Bookmarks, then Add Bookmark, and *voilà*, whatever URL is currently on your screen will be added permanently to your bookmark collection—yours forever until you delete it. (URLs in Go are not saved. When you turn Netscape off, everything in Go will be gone.) As you walk the Web, you will find sites to which you will want to return again and again. Bookmarks allows you to save your favorite URLs for quick and easy access. (On a PC the Bookmarks menu is found in the Location Toolbar, on a Mac it is found in the pull-down menus at the top of your screen.) My bookmark collection is very large, and with the newer browsers it is really easy to organize. Just mouse over to Communicator on the Navigation toolbar and click on Bookmarks. You will see your list of bookmarks. You can organize them into folders and then sort them in any order you wish. Bookmarks is as nifty a time-saver as Stop.

Right next to Bookmarks is another time-saving icon. When you are on a Web page that you want to include in your bookmark list, click on this little icon and it will capture the URL. Now drag that icon with your mouse to the bookmark list, and you can place it in the correct folder. It's a way to organize your bookmarks on the fly.

The Go To, or Location, box is located next to bookmarks. This box displays the URL where you are right now, or you can type the URL of the next page you want to go to. In this way, it has the same function as the Open button.

The What's Related button is new. Click on this button to find out other Web sites that are related to the Web site you are on now. If you want to turn off this feature, go to Edit/Preferences, click on Navigator, and go to Smart Browsing.

The Personal Toolbar

This is a completely programmable toolbar. Here you can put in your most-visited Web sites. I have my personal toolbar set up to the Web sites that I use most frequently. It's a time saver. You can set your personal toolbar any way you like it.

Microsoft Internet Explorer

If you are using Internet Explorer, this is the section for you! Like Netscape Navigator, Internet Explorer is a collection of pull-down menus and toolbars.

Pull-Down Menus

File: Important features include New, to open up a new screen; Open, to open up a new page in the browser (just type in the URL); Save As, which allows you to save the page and the graphics on your hard drive for offline browsing; and Send, which lets you send the link you are visiting to another person via e-mail. Also included are Work Offline (so you can) and Close. Again, you should always know how to exit a program.

Edit: Important features are Cut, Copy, Paste and Select All, as well as Find. Find allows you to find words or phrases on the Web page you are currently on.

View: There are many features on this menu, but for starters, focus on Go To, which is a list of the URLs you have visited this trip on the Web; Source allows you to see the HTML coding on a Web page (important for Chapter 4); and Text Size, which you can change from small to largest.

Favorites: These are the Web sites that you want to visit again and again. To add to your Favorites, click on Favorites, then Add. A window pops up and gives you some choices as to where you want put that URL in your Favorite list. You can put it in a folder and you can also make it available for offline browsing.

Tools will take you to the built-in e-mail program in Internet Explorer. It will also let you synchronize data, so you can view Web pages while offline. Click on Related Links, and a list of links that are related to the Web pages on the screen will appear in a frame to the left of the screen. Lastly, Internet Options is in Tools. This is where you can create your preferences so Internet Explorer will work the way you want it to work.

When you click on Internet Options, a screen appears with tabs labeled General, Security, Content, Connections, Programs and Advanced. On the General tab you can choose the home page (the first page you see when you open the browser). Remember this, as you might want to change the home page to match your lessons.

Also on the General tab is the link for Temporary Internet Files. These files should be deleted regularly so the browser can work efficiently. Just click on Delete Files and the job is done.

History is located on the General tab too. With History you can view the Web pages you have visited for the last several days. Put in the number of "days" you want to keep in the window. If you want to clear History, click on that button.

The *Security* tab lets you control the amount of accessibility you need. Click on the Content tab, and you can set up filters to screen or censor Web pages. The Connections tab is where you set up information about your server or ISP. The Programs tab allows you to set up news groups and the last tab, Advanced, lets you set up details on how you can view Web pages. Look at all of these Internet Options and set them to meet your needs. If you don't like the set up you created, you can always restore the defaults.

The last pull-down menu is *Help*. If you were once a Netscape user, there are tips for you.

There are at least two tool bars in Internet Explorer. Most of the buttons are repeats of items found in the pull-down menus, and most are self-explanatory. Search lets you program your favorite search device, so you do not have to type in the URL.

Netscape vs. Internet Explorer

Both browser programs do the same thing. Both programs look alike, too. There are some features Netscape has that Internet Explorer does not have, and vice versa. What follows is a chart of some Netscape and Internet Explorer terms and their equivalents in the other browser program. All the other "key words" are the same.

Netscape	Internet Explorer
Bookmarks	Favorites
Preferences	Internet Options
Cache	Temporary Internet Files
Reload	Refresh

Opening Your First Web Page

"Half the fun of going is getting there," say the tourist agencies. Now that you know how to have fun getting there, where is it, exactly, that you are going? Your Web-walking destinations include just some of the millions of Web pages out there. They are front doors to libraries of knowledge and they are just a URL away.

Let's Web-walk over to one of the most famous addresses in America, 1600 Pennsylvania Avenue, Washington, D.C.: The White House. Remember, in a browser, the address is called a Uniform Resource Locator or URL (sometimes pronounced "earl"), and it is written in a completely different format. In the location line type in this URL: **http://www.whitehouse.gov/** (note that there are no spaces in this address—URLs do not contain spaces—and it's in all lowercase letters—also very important, as URLs are "case sensitive"). In a few seconds, you will see a picture of the White House and you're in! (No security checks and no waiting in line. This is access!) After the greeting (which changes according to the time of day), and the picture of the White House (which also changes according to the time of day), scroll to the eight buttons: President and Vice President, Citizen's Handbook, Virtual Library, Help Desk, What's New, White House History and Tours, Briefing Room, and White House for Kids. Click on any of these buttons and be treated to what is happening at the White House. I especially like the History and Tours button, as it gives a brief biography of each of the presidents and first ladies. The White House for Kids button leads to a lot of information, too. Click away on the different buttons and see what happens. Click on any of the links and away you go— Forward and Back, click and surf. You've got the idea! Cool!

Scroll down that page and you will see that some words and images are underlined or written in a different color. Click on these underlined/colored links, and you will be automatically transported to a related Web site. The first time I did this, I was already thinking: "This home page is going to make a great lesson for my class!" By the way, these are called *hypertext links*, and the Web is a collection of millions of hypertext links that connect your computer to computers all over the world.

By pointing and clicking in your browser, you have already become a Web-walker. You can point and click along these hypertext hotlinks to millions of home pages. Since thousands are being added daily, you have unlimited opportunities for finding great teaching materials.

Try another Web site. Click on Open, and type in this URL: **http:// www.ceismc.gatech.edu/busyt/** for the Busy Teacher Home Page. Here you will find links to resources related to Archaeology, Art, Astronomy, Biology, Chemistry, Computer Technology, Ecology/Environment, Elementary School, English, Geology, High School Guidance and Counseling, History, Mathematics, Paleontology, Physics, Recess, Sciences (Other), Social Studies, and a Teachers' Reference Section. Carolyn Cole, who designed this Web site, wanted to provide teachers with an easy-to-use source for materials, lesson plans, and classroom activities. This Web site is easy to understand, so it is great for the Internet beginner and a time-saver for the Internet pro.

If you love pets, try NetPets. Click on Open, type in **http:// www.netpets.com/**. I prefer the Godiva Chocolates home page myself at **http://www.godiva.com/**, but alas, I'm not sure if it has any curricular value.

You have just typed in a few URLs and you may be wondering why they have to be so long and complex. With so many new Web sites being added each week—and each one needing a unique URL, or address—they have to be long so they can be different. Once you know how to decode the letters and numbers of URLs, however, they become easier to cope with and remember. If you visit my home page at California State University, Chico (**http:// www.csuchico.edu/educ/egc.html**), you will be greeted with a picture of me, as well as my teaching schedule for the current semester. Let's decode the URL:

http:// tells the computer to search the World Wide Web for hypertext documents. Since most URLs start with **http://**, this is the default mode, which means you do not have to type **http://** when typing a URL which starts with **http://**.

www.csuchico.edu tells the computer to look for a Web site at a server called **csuchico** (short for California State University, Chico) in the **.edu** (dot e-d-u) domain. There are seven main domains and about 100 minor domains.

/educ/ is the folder or path where the Web Page is located on that particular server.

egc is the name of the particular file located in the folder. Since my name is Eileen Giuffré Cotton, I used my initials instead of the whole name. This makes the URL easier to type.

.html says the document is written in hypertext markup language and is therefore readable by a Web browser.

You are probably now wondering what I'm talking about. I'll try again. All documents on the Web are written in a code called HTML (Hypertext Markup Language). HTML lets you follow the links (or underlined or colored words and phrases) on a document to go to another document. These links allow you to move from one location on the Web to another at the click of your mouse. Therefore, an address that begins with **http://** is one that is written in HTML, which may include links to other pages on the Web. You may have noticed that when you see URLs on television and magazine ads, they usually look like "**http:// www.bigcompanyname.com/**." Well, now with either Netscape or Internet Explorer, all you have to do is type in **bigcompanyname**, and the browser will add the rest. Pretty cool!

Every piece of information on the Internet is on a computer (server) somewhere in the world, and every computer has a name. That name can be a word or a number. The name of the computer for my university is **csuchico**, and since I teach at California State University, Chico, that name makes sense to me.

Finally there is the domain, or suffix, or area of specialization, of the server. There are many different domains, all of which represent the type of organization or business that the server does. These domains are written using a dot "." and three letters. "Dot e-d-u" (**.edu**) stands for higher education, and that describes my university. Other domains include **.gov** for government; **.com** for commercial; **.k12** for K–12 education; **.org** for nonprofit organization; **.net** for network; and **.mil** for military. There are a total of 37 different domains, but those listed above are the most common. Sometimes if I know how to decode a URL, I can determine if it is a good source of information for lessons. For school purposes, I look for Web sites in four domains, as they tend to have more accurate information, fewer advertisements and are generally safer for children. My four favorite domains are **.edu**, **.k12**, **.gov**, and **.org**. For example, I feel the information from a Web site developed by educators is more unbiased, more accurate, and more child-safe than a Web site developed by a commercial operation. While this is not always the case, it is one of the rules of thumb I follow. This will make more sense as you surf the Web. Honest!

In addition to domains or suffixes, some Web sites also tell their country of origin. These are denoted by a state and/or country abbreviation after the domain. Thus, **.jp** means the computer is in Japan, or **.mn.us** means the computer is in Minnesota, in the United States. The state and country domains use the same abbreviations as the Post Office.

What to Do When You Don't Get to Where You Want to Go

Sometimes when you are browsing the Web, you are met by one of a dismaying array of negative responses. Among these are "403 Forbidden," "404 Not Found," and "Unable to connect to host."

Wow! How can something on the Internet be forbidden? If you get that warning, you are being told that you need to have a subscription, membership, or password to access the site. Sometimes these are free sites, sometimes you have to pay, and sometimes you have to belong to a certain organization. No matter what, you will need to register for the site in order to open it up. After you register, you will be given a password (which you must remember) to access the Web site again. No password, no go.

The "Not Found" message may indicate that the targeted Web site has moved to another location, has changed its name and URL, has disappeared, or your Internet provider cannot find the location. When you get this message, try again in a little while and it might be found. If it still is not found, then you might have to use a search engine to find the new URL, if one exists.

"Unable to Connect" means the site is probably busy, just like your telephone is busy once in a while. If you try at another time, you might be able to connect. At the beginning of the semester when all the students are back on campus, I get the Unable to Connect message often because all the lines are busy! Once school has been in session about a month, the message rarely appears.

Sometimes you may have trouble getting a URL to work. If so, truncate the address—don't type the whole thing, backing up a segment at a time from the right-hand side—and try it again. For example, if you cannot get to **http://www.csuchico.edu/educ/ egc.html**, delete **egc.html** and press ENTER. If that does not work, then delete **/educ/** and press ENTER again. When you get to the "server.domain" section of the URL, you will get to the computer where the Web page resides. However, there is still no guarantee that the Web page is still there.

Sometimes nothing seems to work. Your computer seems to be getting clogged up, everything's down, and your browser just cranks and cranks away, but goes nowhere. That's when it's time to do one of two things: Clear the Cache or pull the plug. To clear the cache, go to the Preferences/Advanced/Cache (for Netscape), or Internet Options/General/Temporary Internet Files (for Internet Explorer). Click on the appropriate button and erase the cache/temporary files. The Cache/Temporary Files is a collection of many of the documents and graphics that you have viewed on the Web. Since you may often revisit some Web sites, your browser saves images and documents you frequently request on the hard drive of your computer. This saves a lot of time. Imagine your computer downloading a new copy of the Yahoo logo every time you do a search. However when the Cache/Temporary Files gets full, it slows down the browser. When this happens, click on the Clear Cache Now/Delete Temporary Files button and the file will be emptied. If your cache was full, then the speed of the computer and browser will be back to normal. If that does not work, and your browser still seems to be S-L-O-W, log out, get out of Windows or restart your computer. When you fire it up again; it'll probably work. I know this sounds strange, but the Web and browsers are not user-friendly 100% of the time!

Surfing the Net or Mining the Web?

Now that you know how to ring the bells and blow the whistles, it's time to play a tune. Web-walk with abandon—play with the buttons and pull-down menus to find out what they do! See what you can find! Let the kid in you come out—go ahead, you can't break the machine, or wreck the program (well, *probably* not)! You'll be surprised at how easy it is to use these comprehensive, Web-embracing browsers. See for yourself what you think of this tool for exploring the resources on the Internet. There is a difference, by the way, between surfing the net and mining the Web. Surfing is having fun, while mining is researching the Web to find specific information. Right now, surf. When you become more adept at using the Internet, start mining gems of information from it.

The beauty of most browsers is their similarity. Most have nearly identical functions, although the terminology for their buttons and options may differ. Netscape and Internet Explorer are the cool browsers this week—but next year? Who knows? I contend that if you have worked with either one of these browsers, you will be able to work with the newer browsers as they are developed. After you walk around the Internet for awhile, you will start to click on connecting links and get to worlds and places you did not believe existed. When you start getting serious about using this tool for learning, you are no longer surfing the Internet, you are mining the Web for information. This is the serious business you want to involve your students in doing. This is where you start learning and using information gleaned from various Web sites.

Why don't you give this a try. In your browser, type in **http://ericir.syr.edu** and you will visit ERIC (Educational Resources Information Center), the publisher of this book. Here you can find many useful resources for school and home. This might start out as a surfing trip and end up being a mining expedition.

Most of the chapters in this book have a built-in lesson. In this chapter, I offer you no other lesson plan than this: After you have surfed the Web for awhile, it might be time to take your newfound knowledge to your classroom and demonstrate the power of the Internet to your students. Don't be amazed if they know more than you do! They have the time to surf and learn, while you do not. Show them some of the things you have discovered thus far, and then listen to the discussion. Learn from them, and also share your excitement and amazement with them. Give them a Web-walking tour and, if you are brave (and have the equipment), a set of URLs for them to explore. This is a tough lesson to evaluate, but you should be able to see eyes wide open with wonder and fascination. And you'll hear lots of noise! If you see and hear the above, the lesson was successful!

Disclaimer Statement

The Web is a living, growing, rapidly changing thing. There's no guarantee that a Web site you found yesterday will still be there tomorrow. Likewise, there is no guarantee that the Web sites that I recommend in this book will necessarily still be there when you try to find them. That's another reason to have the URL for this book on your bookmark list. Please help me out. If you should see that one of the Web sites in this book is no longer working, write to me at **cotton@instruction.com** and tell me about it. The next time I update the Web page, I'll change that URL. As a reminder, the Web page for the book is **http://www.csuchico.edu/ online_classroom**.

Happy Web-walking!

Chapter 2
A Wealth of Web Sites

The Web has millions of pages of non-cataloged information, and finding the information you are seeking is sometimes impossible. However, if you have a few places to start, the job gets easier. This chapter will give you over a hundred of the best sources of information for teaching with the Internet. Each of the Web sites has been evaluated for authority (who is responsible for the Web site), accuracy and currency of information, objective and thorough coverage of information, and ease of use. Some of the Web sites contain ready-made lesson plans. Others supply you with the information you need to design goal-oriented lessons that meet your objectives. Still others will give you information about the latest trends in integrating Internet technology into your classroom. Unlike journals or books, the Web sites are free, so click on Open and start typing in URLs, or go to **http://www.csuchico.edu/Online_Classroom** and click on Chapter 2.

General K–12 Resources

⊙ Kathy Schrock's Guide for Educators

http://school.discovery.com/schrockguide/

Kathy has been working on this Web site for years, and it keeps getting better. Here you can find resources for every curriculum area, easy-to-find search engines and directories, lessons about using the Internet, slide shows you can use for training, and more. It is truly an amazing Web site, and one you need to keep going back to time and again. This Web site is updated daily, so the information is always current.

⊙ Teacher Pathfinder: Educational Village

http://teacherpathfinder.org/

This Web site was recommended to me by a teacher. It has a colorful resource list that is an extensive information source. Click on the Schoolhouse for a great list of tools you can use in the classroom.

⊙ ED's Oasis K–12 Resources

http://www.edsoasis.org/

The mission of this Web page is simple: "To help teachers use the Internet as an integral tool for teaching and learning," and it meets it's mission statement. Click on Treasure Zone and you will see high-quality, student-centered lessons that are designed by teachers and aligned to meet curriculum standards. ED's Oasis is very particular. To be listed here, your Web site must meet strict criteria.

PageSpider's Teacher Page

http://www.pagespider.com/Teachers/

Peter Harris, a teacher and computer specialist, has designed this page with you in mind. The list of resources keeps getting better and his categories are fantastic. Check out the following: Associations, Searches and Collections, Science, Music, Mathematics, Literature, Storytelling and Theatre, Education Technology, Teaching Materials, Lesson Plans & Resources, Shareware and Freeware Collections, and Hot Links for Teachers.

Classroom Connect: The G.R.A.D.E.S. Archive

http://www.classroom.net/grades/

The main Classroom Connect site can be found at **http://www.classroom.net/**. However, the G.R.A.D.E.S. Archive is what you really want. It is a hand-picked collection of over 850 quality education-related Internet sites. The Web sites are categorized by topic and grade level. This Web site is updated often—these people are serious about teaching with the Internet! I like to stop at Classroom Connect and find out where their next Connected Classroom Conference is going to be, as well as find out what Internet projects they are sponsoring.

Education World: Where Educators Go to Learn

http://www.education-world.com/

At Education World there are over 110,000 resources available to you. You can read the current news about integrating the Internet into your classroom, find lessons, join a discussion group, read book reviews, and generally "get caught up" on all that you need to know about teaching with and without the Internet.

◗ McRel Internet Connections

http://www.mcrel.org/resources/links/

McRel stands for Mid-continent Regional Educational Laboratory, one of several regional labs across the country. (Check out all of the Regional Labs at **http://www.nwrel.org/national/**.) The folks at McRel rely on educators to give them the best online educational resources available. McRel provides federally-funded services to Colorado, Kansas, Missouri, Nebraska, North Dakota, South Dakota, and Wyoming.

◗ Filamentality

http://www.kn.pacbell.com/wired/fil/

helping you add your own Filament to the web of learning

Don't know exactly how to use the Internet in your classroom? Go to Filamentality and this interactive Web site will guide you through picking a topic, searching the Web, gathering good Internet sites, and turning Web resources into activities appropriate for your kids. A great site for beginners and experts alike!

◗ NetLearning: Why Teachers Use the Internet

http://www.songline.com/teachers/index.html

This is a Web site for teachers who want to foster online learning. Here you can find out how to teach with the Internet with one computer and a modem. There is also a wealth of topics to read about including Acceptable Use Policies, Internet filtering (or censoring) programs, educational technology, grant resources, online projects and student publications, as well as resources on animals and insects, geography, the arts, government, languages, literature, math, and science. There is a "Top Ten List" of reasons teachers use the Internet. While the Web page does not meet all of my criteria, some of the information it contains is timeless.

⦿ Pacific Bell Blue Web'n

http://www.kn.pacbell.com/wired/bluewebn/

Pacific Bell has collected a library of "blue ribbon" learning sites on the Internet. Read some of the best lessons, resources, activities and projects available in Science, English, Math, History, Art, Business and more. Scroll down to the Applications Table and be treated to some of the best Internet resources around. Each one has been screened using their complex evaluation rubric found at **http://www.kn.pacbell.com/wired/bluewebn/ rubric.html**. This is also a helpful rubric to keep in mind when evaluating student Web-design work. If you want to be on their mailing list, they will send you a list of the new additions to the Web site each week. It's a very handy reminder of all the good resources that are available.

⦿ K–12 Sources - Curriculum - Lessons Plans

http://execpc.com/~dboals/k-12.html

One of my students found this page. She said "Eileen, you won't believe all the stuff on it." And she was right! When I first started going to this Web site, there were only 185 links to sites of an educational nature. Now there are too many to count. This mini-directory has everything from the Virtual Frog Dissection Kit to Music. If you want to find something specific on it, use the Find button in your browser. "The major purpose of this home page is to encourage the use of the World Wide Web as a tool for learning and teaching and to provide some help for K–12 classroom teachers in locating and using the resources of the Internet in the classroom." That's something I believe in! If you check out all the resources listed, you will never leave your computer.

⦿ The TradeWave Galaxy

http://www.einet.net/galaxy.html

galaxy   *The professional's guide to a world of information.*

I'm not sure if this is a general directory, the index to an encyclopedia, or what. This site includes hundreds of links to Arts & Humanities, Business and Commerce, Community, Engineering and Technology, Government, Law, Leisure & Recreation, Medicine, Reference and Interdisciplinary Sources, Science, and Social Science. Each link leads you to topics that can be used in your curriculum. By the way, Education resources are listed on this site, almost at the bottom—click on Find and you will be taken there straight away.

⦿ Sholom's Resources for Students and Teachers

http://members.home.com/sholom/pub/
ResourceTables.html

Sholom has found resources for his students in six major areas: Education, Humanities, The Sciences, Computer Technology, Mother Earth, and Miscellaneous. It has an easy-to-use matrix that my students seem to like and, if you have questions, you can e-mail Sholom, who is more than helpful. Don't forget to check out the Canadiana box.

◯ Teachers Helping Teachers

http://pacificnet.net/~mandel/index.html

The purpose of this site is threefold: 1) provide basic teaching tips to inexperienced teachers—ideas that can be immediately implemented in the classroom; 2) provide new ideas in teaching methodologies for all teachers; and 3) provide a forum for experienced teachers to share their expertise with colleagues around the world. A chat area for teachers is included and there is a great list of educational resources. Updates are added each week during the school year.

◯ The Global Schoolhouse

http://www.gsn.org/

This Web site claims to link kids, teachers, and parents around the world. They focus on using communications technologies to support learning. Click on Projects to see if there is one you want to join. Click on Link-o-Rama to a catalog of links recommended by teachers.

Welcome to: **THE GLOBAL SCHOOLHOUSE**

◯ The Teacher's Desk

http://mycroft.mexia.com/~judihar/tdesk2.html

Judy Hardison was a teacher and she has an unusual (and slightly sarcastic) sense of humor. I like this page. It is not the usual list of links (although a list is there, you just have to look for it). At this site you can read about her twist on the traditional curriculum and how to use the Internet to enhance it. She updates it about twice a year.

Web66: A K–12 World Wide Web Project
http://web66.coled.umn.edu/

Web66 is supposed to conjure up thoughts of Route 66 by taking you on a virtual tour of what's available for teachers on the Internet. I think it succeeds. The College of Education at the University of Minnesota houses this fantastic site. With topics in Education, Technology, and Information, you are bound to find something useful. I like "Mustang" as well as the Web66 Cookbook for HTML, but those are only two of many excellent selections available.

Web Sites and Resources for Teachers
http://www.csun.edu/~vceed009/

Drs. Vicki and Richard Sharp are teachers at California State University, Northridge (a sister campus to my California State University, Chico), who have collected Web sites and put them into eight categories: Language Arts, Social Studies, Math, Science, Art, Music, Just for Kids, and ESL/Bilingual. When you click on one of the categories, you are greeted with an annotated list of Web sites related to that topic. This is a well-organized site that's maintained regularly, so there is rarely a dead link. I like that!

700+ Great Sites
http://www.ala.org/parentspage/greatsites/amazing.html

Compiled by a division of the American Library Association, this Web site actively looks for resources that are "amazing, spectacular, mysterious, and colorful for kids and the adults who care about them." Look at the two major categories: 1) Sites for Kids and 2) Sites for Parents, Caregivers, Teachers, and Others who Care for Kids.

⬤ Integrating the Internet

http://seamonkey.ed.asu.edu/~hixson/index/index5.html

Still confused about integrating the Internet into your teaching? Look at this page by Susan Hixson. See lessons and resources that have been used and work well in the classroom.

⬤ Encarta: Schoolhouse

http://encarta.msn.com/schoolhouse/default.asp?tr=181

Microsoft has created a depository for lesson plans at Schoolhouse. Click on the subject area and you will soon be greeted with several lesson plans. Even if I do not like the lesson plan, I have been given an idea that might make a good lesson plan for me.

Federal and State Education Web sites

⬤ U.S. Department of Education

http://www.ed.gov/

Probably the first governmental department you need to visit is the Department of Education at the Federal level. Read the mission statement of the Department of Education and the National Educational Goals, access education guides, and find out about education initiatives and grant opportunities. Here you can also read the latest information about bills in Congress that will affect education. It's always nice to know what is going to happen and how it might affect you. You can also find out information about the E-Rate, a way to fund Internet access to your school.

The Departments of Education in just about every state and U.S. territory have posted huge resource pages with lots of links they think will be helpful to educators about state curriculum requirements and credentialing laws. To find a list of all governmental sites, check out the Piper List at **http://www.piperinfo.com/ state/states.html**. Here you will find a clickable list of states and territories that will lead you to all the governmental services of that geographical area. The next task is to scroll down to the education listing.

If that list is too cumbersome, I've listed a few state Departments of Education that might be helpful. This is just a sampling of states, so your state might not be mentioned.

⬤ Colorado Department of Education

http://www.cde.state.co.us/

There is specific information about Colorado here, but everyone should click on Electronic Resources and Information and Interesting Sites for Students, Teachers and Others.

⬤ California Department of Education Goldmine

http://goldmine.cde.ca.gov/

This site has California curriculum frameworks, California legislation as it relates to schools and education, and links to lesson plans and other resources.

⬤ The Texas Education Network (TENET)

http://www.tenet.edu/

Texans do things in a big way, so this is a big site. If you are a registered TENET user, the whole site is accessible. If not, you can browse TENET but you might not be able to access everything. You can also check out the Texas Education Agency at **http://www.tea.texas.gov/**.

● Indiana Department of Education

http://doe.state.in.us/

Indiana has a good set of links to other Departments of Education as well as resources, Acceptable Use Policies and standards.

● New York State Education Department

http://www.nysed.gov/

At this Web site, I particularly like the Resource Guides and the Current News, but other information about state licensing, graduation requirements, etc. are included.

And Now a Word from ERIC (Educational Resources Information Center)

● Ask ERIC

http://ericir.syr.edu/

ERIC is a federally-funded national information database. It has sixteen subject-specific clearinghouses that provide a variety of services and products on education-related issues. Check out the virtual library and the ERIC digests.

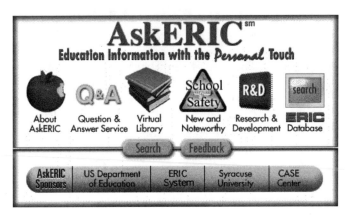

⬤ ERIC Clearinghouse on Reading, English, and Communication

http://www.indiana.edu/~eric_rec/index.html

Clearinghouse on Reading, English, and Communication

ERIC/REC is one of the sixteen clearinghouses, and they are the people who publish this book. At this site you can find bibliographies and research summaries, search the ERIC database, ask questions of the ERIC/REC user-services team, and find out about professional development workshops in your area.

⬤ AskERIC Educational Question and Answer Service

http://ericir.syr.edu/Qa/

Do you have a question about education? Are you a parent, teacher, librarian or anyone else interested in education? If so, then Ask ERIC the question and within forty-eight hours you will receive an answer. This service works!

Science and Math Resources

General Resources

⬤ The Discovery Channel School

http://school.discovery.com/

The goal of The Discovery Channel School is to provide innovative online materials for teachers and students, using the resources of Discovery Channel, The Learning Channel, Animal Planet, and the Travel Channel. They provide lesson plans, classroom activities, online expeditions, and special features to support curriculum commonly taught in schools. I had a chance to work with these people two years ago on one of their programs and I was impressed at the thoroughness they demanded.

○ The Eisenhower National Clearinghouse for Math and Science

http://www.enc.org/nf_index.htm (no frames)
http://www.enc.org/ (frames)

This is a milestone Web site as far as I'm concerned. Here you can find wonderful activities to use in your classroom that have been written by teachers for students. Check out the math sites, the best school sites, and Internet tools for parents.

○ SAMI (Science and Math Initiatives)

http://www.learner.org/sami/.

I have found that math-related sites are difficult to find, but SAMI has some. The "Chatback Line," "Mathematics and Science Curricula," "Other Resources," and "Rural Resources" are all worth viewing. Click on Lesson Plans and Projects, and find a list of links to both math and science.

○ The Why Files: The Science Behind the News

http://whyfiles.news.wisc.edu/

This online newspaper tries to explain the science behind the headlines. Web-walk here and click on more stories from previous issues, sports images and science, a cool science image, a search engine for the Web site, and a Q/A forum.

○ Frank Potter's Science Gems

http://www-sci.lib.uci.edu/SEP/SEP.html

Frank Potter and Jim Martindale mine the Web to find the best science sites for teachers. Currently the collection consists of 2,000 sites and more are being added on a regular basis. The site is annotated and categorized according to grade level and there is a weekly update.

◯ You Can with Beakman and Jax

http://www.beakman.com

This is the Web site for the television series *Beakman's Place*.
Check out the question-and-answer section, see pictures from the Hubble Telescope, get a Web-based Periodic Table of Elements, and just mine this site for fun and valuable information.

◯ Windows to the Universe

http://www.windows.umich.edu/

The University of Michigan wanted to develop a fun and different Web site about Earth and Space Sciences. A challenging Web site that stretches your brain.

◯ Access Excellence

http://www.accessexcellence.org/index.html

This Web site was launched in 1993 to provide high-school biology teachers and other scientists access to new scientific information using the World Wide Web. The Web site is funded by Genentech, Inc. Read What's New, About Biotech, About Teaching Communities, Activities Exchange (see mystery spot for some fun lessons), Let's Collaborate, and Classrooms for the 21st Century. Good information that is updated regularly, with lots of activities you can adapt to your middle or high school biology classes.

Planets and Space

● NASA Home Page

http://www.nasa.gov/NASA_homepage.html/

NASA NASA (National Aeronautics and Space Administration) offers a wealth of goodies for teachers and students, and there are links to many other sites of scientific interest. There are also other excellent NASA sites on the Web, including the Mars Global Surveyor (**http://mars.jpl.nasa.gov/mgs/**), Earth Observatory (**http://mars.jpl.nasa.gov/mgs/**), Human Space Flight (**http://spaceflight.nasa.gov/index-m.html**) and more. There are many graphics at these sites, so they do take more time to load.

● The Messier Science Page

http://seds.lpl.arizona.edu/messier/Messier.html

From 1758 to 1782, Charles Messier, a French astronomer, compiled a list of a hundred diffuse objects that he thought were comets. As it turned out, the "comets" were nebulae, star clusters, and other beautiful objects found in the night sky. The study of these objects by astronomers has lead to important, incredible discoveries such as the life cycles of stars, the reality of galaxies as separate "island universes," and the possible age of the universe. Go to this site to see some excellent graphics on the wonders of the night sky.

● The Nine Planets: A Multimedia Tour of Our Solar System

http://seds.lpl.arizona.edu/billa/tnp/

At this comprehensive examination of our solar system, you will find links to just about everything now known about our nine planets: moons, orbits, the Hubble telescope and its photos of outer space, and much more.

◐ Welcome to the Planets

http://pds.jpl.nasa.gov/planets/

A tour of our Solar System from the Jet Propulsion Lab and the California Institute of Technology. This site goes along well with the Nine Planets Web site.

◐ Ocean Planet Home Page

http://seawifs.gsfc.nasa.gov/ocean-planet.html

This Smithsonian exhibit looks at the power of the ocean. To quote them, "it plumbs the depths of the watery world" . . . but I wouldn't want to go that far. The many facets of this site will take some time to explore.

Life Science

◐ The National Geographic

http://www.nationalgeographic.com/kids/

This Web site is similar to the magazine. There are links to articles as well as fun and games.

◐ The Heart: An Online Demonstration

http://sln2.fi.edu/biosci/heart.html

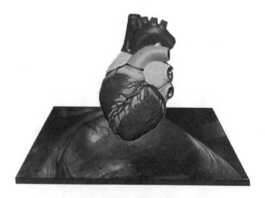

This is a fantastic lesson about the heart and the circulatory system. I have shared this Web site with many teachers who have created lessons based on it. It is a natural for upper elementary curriculum. While you are here, click on the home page for this Web site and find the Franklin Institute Science Museum at **http://www.fi.edu/**. You will not be disappointed.

● Science Learning Network

http://www.sln.org/

Once you get to this science site, which is devoted to inquiry, click on Resources and find lessons about water, hurricanes, the wind, and the Cow's Eye dissection.

SCIENCE LEARNING NETWORK
www.sln.org

● The Invention Dimension

http://web.mit.edu/invent/

I don't know if this is a science Web site or a history Web site. I do know it's interesting and kids seem to enjoy finding out about the people who invented stuff and stories behind the invention. There is a different inventor featured each week, too.

● The Cow's Eye Dissection

http://www.exploratorium.edu/learning_studio/cow_eye/

Along with a step-by-step lesson on the anatomy of a cow's eye, there is a short audio introduction with laughing kids and statements such as "Gross!" But hang in there—the purpose of this anatomy lesson is to learn more about how the eye works. While you are here, click on the Eye Primer.

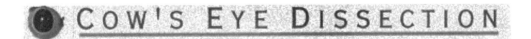

● COW'S EYE DISSECTION

◉ The Visible Human Project

http://www.nlm.nih.gov/research/visible/visible_human.html

The idea of this project is to create a three-dimensional view of a human male and a human female. Although quite complex, this site is very interesting. The Web site requires a browser that can interpret Java. Check out the Medline for health information at this location.

◉ Virtual Frog Dissection Kit

http://george.lbl.gov/ITG.hm.pg.docs/dissect/info.html

The University of California at Berkeley and the Lawrence Livermore Labs offer a good way to familiarize your students with the anatomy of the frog, without having to breathe formaldehyde or handle a dead amphibian (a major disappointment, I admit, to a true-hearted future biologist). The Dissection Kit is a superb application of virtual reality to classroom learning.

Pre-History

◉ Honolulu Community College Dinosaur Exhibit

http://www.hcc.hawaii.edu/dinos/dinos.1.html

Dinosaurs in Hawaii? Yes. This great museum exhibit has pictures of dinosaurs, as well as a guided audio tour. While the page was last updated in 1996, dinosaurs have been extinct for far longer.

⬤ Archeology Resources for Education

http://www.interlog.com/~jabram/elise/archres.htm

I find that most kids like digging around, and thus archeology can be quite fascinating. For a comprehensive listing about archeology, check out what the Royal Ontario Museum has to offer.

Sports Science

⬤ Science of Sport

http://www.exploratorium.edu/sports/index.html

Learn about the science behind hockey, baseball, and cycling. Learn facts about fitness, the physical mechanics of the sport, reaction time, and energy. This multimedia Web site uses video clips and interviews of scientists and players, all talking about their craft. There are many lessons that can be derived from this Web site. While you are there, go to the home page of The Exploratorium at **http://www.exploratorium.edu/** for lessons and games that relate to science, art, and human perception.

Math

○ The Math Forum Home Page

http://forum.swarthmore.edu/index.js.html

Located at Swarthmore College, The Math Forum has a compendium of lists for students, teachers, and researchers. It also features what is new and exciting in the world of mathematics. Here you can join a Math Forum, gather valuable resources at the Internet Mathematics Library (**http://forum.swarthmore.edu/library/**) as well as lesson plans at **http://forum.swarthmore.edu/library/resource_types/lesson_plans/**. A must-see for math teachers at all grade levels. You can also "Ask Dr. Math" while you are here at **http://forum.swarthmore.edu/dr.math/**.

○ Interactive Mathematics Online

http://tqd.advanced.org/2647/main.htm

Algebra, Geometry, Trigonometry, Chaos Theory, and Make your own Stereograms are some of the resources offered here. Check out cool math sites at **http://tqd.advanced.org/2647/mathrefs.htm**.

○ The Math Virtual Library: General Resources

http://euclid.math.fsu.edu/Science/General.html

Here are over sixty math and science links. Some of them are good, others I would skip. Peruse the list and see which links fit your needs.

◉ Fractals

http://math.rice.edu/~lanius/frac/

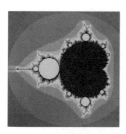

Cynthia Lanius has designed a fractals unit for elementary and middle school math students that is fun and informative. Another Web site on this topic is The Fractal Microscope at **http://www.ncsa.uiuc.edu/Edu/Fractal/ Fractal_Home.html**. These two Web sites complement each other well.

◉ Welcome to Mega-Math

http://www.c3.lanl.gov/mega-math/menu.html (text)
http://www.c3.lanl.gov/mega-math/index.html (image map)

The Los Alamos Lab has devised and collected Web sites that will help explain mathematical phenomena such as graphing, machines, infinity, knots, and ice cream.

Language Arts Resources

General Collections

◉ The Children's Literature Web Guide

http://www.ucalgary.ca/~dkbrown/index.html

The Children's Literature Web Guide

This excellent Web site offers all sorts of links to good children's literature. There are also links for teachers, parents, storytellers, and kids. I like "Authors on the Web" at **http://www.acs.ucalgary.ca/~dkbrown/authors.html** and the recent winners of Newbery and Caldecott awards.

● Carol Hurst's Children's Literature Site

http://www.carolhurst.com/

See a collection of reviews of books for kids, ways to use them in the classroom and collections of books and activities about particular subjects, curriculum areas, themes and professional topics. Look for the curriculum units that integrate literature into history and science.

● Fairrosa CyberLibrary

http://www.dalton.org/libraries/fairrosa/

This is a list of links that leads to classics, fairy and folk tales, stories and rhymes, and magazines. I've used this list to find books for several classes and have not struck out yet. A collection of Lewis Carroll works resides at this Web site. Also check out Authors and Illustrators.

Specific Collections

● Candlelight Stories

http://www.CandlelightStories.com/

Here is a collection of stories from all over the world. Some are old favorites and fairy tales, some have been written by kids. Also included are e-mail cards, spelling games, write to your senator, a classroom writing area, and a place to write book reviews.

⊙ Internet Public Library Story Hour

http://ipl.sils.umich.edu/youth/StoryHour/

Just a link from the larger Internet Public Library Web site, you can read some online stories and look at pictures related to the stories. Some of the stories have RealAudio so your students can hear the story as they read it.

⊙ Animals, Myths & Legends

http://www.ozemail.com.au/~oban/

This site is a collection of recently written myths and legends that look at the relationship between man, animals and the universe. I've used this Web site with several classes, comparing these stories with familiar "western" stories, and to discuss the theme of harmony and living together to create a better world. The Web site is recommended for 3- to 8-year-olds, but I'm sure many people have read the legends and found them intriguing and interesting. It is a family-friendly Web site and "child safe."

⊙ Cinderella Project

http://www-dept.usm.edu/~engdept/cinderella/
cinderella.html
http://www-dept.usm.edu/~engdept/cinderella/
inventory.html

Twelve versions of the Cinderella Story written from 1729 to 1912 are available at this Web site. Here you can compare and contrast the stories to analyze the fairy tale. There are also plans available for individual Cinderella stories as well as a fairly complete bibliography. Here's a series of lessons just waiting to be taught.

○ Mythweb

http://www.mythweb.com/

This is a Web site devoted to the gods, goddesses, heroes, heroines, and monsters of Greek Mythology. Unlike so many "mythology" Web sites, this one does not have a lot of misspellings or misinformation. Find a copy of the Odyssey and an encyclopedia of terms from Greek Mythology.

○ Poetry for Kids

http://www.poetry4kids.com/poems.html

This site is written by a children's poet, Ken Nesbitt. There are always forty funny poems to read here. There are also directions on how to write poetry, and links to other poetry Web sites. The site is updated regularly, so the links work!

○ S.C.O.R.E Language Arts

http://www.sdcoe.k12.ca.us/score/cla.html

This page is put together by the San Diego, California, County Office of Education. Check out the CyberGuides, which are great plans written and tested by teachers. Also look at the resources, which include links to more lesson plans, literature, assessment and more. This Web site is updated regularly.

○ Shakespeare on the Web
The Complete Works of William Shakespeare

http://the-tech.mit.edu/Shakespeare.html

○ Surfing with The Bard
(Your Shakespeare Classroom on the Internet)

http://www.ipl.org/reading/shakespeare/shakespeare.html

If you are studying The Bard, visit any of these Web sites for complete copies of his comedies, tragedies, sonnets, and poems, along with a wonderful interactive glossary. When you are reading the text and you come across a word you do not know, click on it, and the glossary will appear, telling you what the word meant during Shakespeare's time.

Animabets.com

http://www.animabets.com/

A Web site put together by a group of programmers, artists, educators, designers and visionaries who believe that the Internet can be used as a powerful tool for educating kids. There are twenty-six characters (one for each letter) who are part of the collection of stories and each character has an e-mail address. This is great fun if you want to get your kids (ages 5–10) interacting with a story.

Publishing Stories on the Web

Kid's Space

http://www.kids-space.org/

"This place is rated G" according to the banner across the top of the page, and it is another place where kids can show off their writing, painting, and thinking to others. If you are looking to publish your kids' work, search no more.

KidScribe: A Bilingual Site for Kid Authors

http://web2.airmail.net/def/

This page is in both English and Spanish. Your students can publish their own stories at **http://web2.airmail.net/def/ playform.htm**, as well as read stories, poems, and jokes written by other kids.

Culture and Language Resources

The Internet is about communicating with other people. Contrary to the often heard idea that computers depersonalize learning, Internet-connected computers now do more to put learners in contact with other learners—and people with people—than any other communication medium. Help your students achieve global interpersonal dialogue by building keypal (like penpals but using a keyboard instead of a pen) relationships and also by plugging into Web sites that link them to other people and other cultures.

◑ Human Languages Page

http://www.june29.com/HLP/

Tyler Jones is the guru of languages. He improves this page all the time. At this single URL you can find out something about almost every language spoken on earth. Check out the easy ones first, such as Spanish or French, and then try any other language you can think of—Croatian or Basque or Afrikaans—including languages that are no longer spoken, such as Middle English.

◑ Mythology of North American Indians

http://www.windows.umich.edu/cgi-bin/tour.cgi/ worldmap_new_gif.map(sw=false&sn=324991&d=/ mythology&edu=elem&br=graphic&cd=false&fr=f&tour=)?128,121

Sorry about the *long* URL, but this Web site is worth a visit. See links to learn about the Mythology of North American Indians related to objects in the sky, the Earth, and other aspects of their world. You can choose a beginner, intermediate, or advanced level to read. Part of a larger page on World Mythology at **http:// www.windows.umich.edu/cgi-bin/tour.cgi?link=/mythology/ worldmap_new.html&sw=false&sn=324991&d=/ mythology&edu=elem&br=graphic&cd=false&fr=f&tour=**.

◉ Kids Web Japan

http://www.jinjapan.org/kidsweb/

Learn some Japanese legends, find out about today's weather in Japan, go to other great links, and visit virtual Japanese culture. It's a good way to learn a little bit more about Japan.

◉ The Vocabulary Cab

http://members.xoom.com/voccab/

Vocabulary Cab introduces you to new words that you need for school. The page is designed for English Language Learners, but don't let that stop English Language Speakers from playing the Word & Roots Cab or the Quiz Cab.

History and Social Science Resources

General Resources

◉ History Social Science K–12 WebPage

http://www.execpc.com/~dboals/boals.html

You were first introduced to a link from this site under General Resources (remember it included over 250 Web sites). Well, this is the home page, and it is devoted to History and Social Science. I have no idea how many links are in this compendium, but suffice it to say there are scads of them. Another lifelong adventure will be just going through all the Web sites at this one URL. The Web site is updated regularly so the links usually work.

● Mr. Dowling's Virtual Classroom

http://www.mrdowling.com/

This is an online geography book that has been created by Mr. Dowling, a 6th-grade teacher in Florida. Here are his lessons, homework handouts, ideas, and links. The Web site represents all of the geography he teaches throughout the year. It's a great resource for teachers, and a fun way for students to learn geography.

● The Washington State Social Studies Home Page

http://www.learningspace.org/socialstudies/default.html

At this site you can view the guidelines for social studies in Washington state, but even more important are the links to Social Studies-related resources. I especially like the link called "This month in history."

● Social Studies Lesson Plans for Teachers

http://www.csun.edu/%7Ehcedu013/index.html

Dr. Marty Levine has developed this site with social studies teachers in mind. It offers links to lesson plans, resources, online activities, and current events.

● HyperHistory

http://www.hyperhistory.com/online_n2/History_n2/a.html

A collection of historical timelines from before 1000 B.C. to the present time. Click on the time period to find out more about the people, history, events, and maps.

Specific Resources

⬤ Selected Civil War Photographs

http://memory.loc.gov/ammem/cwphome.html

The Library of Congress has 1,118 Civil War photographs made by Mathew Brady or one of his colleagues. Click on Search if you know what you want, click on Browse to see a set of categories. The photos are all black and white and tell a story about this terrible war in American history.

⬤ American Civil War Home Page

http://sunsite.utk.edu/civil-war/

The American Civil War is studied in the fifth, eighth, and tenth or eleventh grades in most districts. Sometimes the battles are recreated. The dry and dusty old history lessons have come to life thanks to a recent PBS documentary. With timelines, maps, documents, diaries written by young and old alike, pictures, and more, this site is a special hit with middle-school teachers. If you teach any aspect of American History, you will want to add this site to your list of bookmarks.

⬤ Welcome to the Civil War Center

http://www.cwc.lsu.edu/

To complement the American Civil War Page, you must see the Civil War Center. These folks have over a thousand links to information about one of the worst wars in America's history. You'll find movie and audio clips, as well as other goodies.

● 1492 Exhibit

http://sunsite.unc.edu/expo/1492.exhibit/Intro.html

This Library of Congress exhibit that follows the 1492 voyage of Christopher Columbus includes maps and graphics.

● Archiving Early America

http://earlyamerica.com/

A collection of documents from the 18th century can be found at this Web site. You can also read about the lives of famous early Americans, join an online forum, find out what happened on this day in early America, and read the freedom papers. If you teach early Americana, this is the Web site you need to visit.

● MapQuest

http://www.mapquest.com/

At this Web site you can get map directions to just about anywhere in the world. I've used it with kids and I've used it to find a specific address in a specific city. This site is amazing. The kids think it's magic and I agree with them. By the way, this Web site has the ability to locate anything . . . even your house. Big Brother is watching!

◉ The Teaching Learning Web

http://www.usgs.gov/education/learnweb/index.html

A set of lessons developed by the U.S.G.S. (U.S. Geological Service) that deal with global change, maps and earth science. I've used the Maps lesson several times and it is a good one!

◉ 50 U.S. States

http://www.50states.com/

If you are teaching the states and capitals, then this is the place to go! Click on each state to find out information about it. This Web site is extensive with over 9000 Web pages. You can also find out information about U.S. territories, other nations in the world, and colleges and universities.

◉ Women in World History Curriculum by Lyn Reese

http://home.earthlink.net/~womenwhist/index.html

This well-maintained Web site is full of interactive information and resources about women's experiences in world history. It is for teachers, teenagers, parents, and history buffs.

◯ Suffrage History

http://www.pbs.org/onewoman/suffrage.html

Mostly text, this PBS site tells the history of women's suffrage. PBS has information and educational pages related to all of its shows at **http://www.pbs.org/**.

◯ The Electronic Embassy

http://www.embassy.org/

The ELECTRONIC
EMBASSY™
*a resource of and for the Washington, D.C.
foreign embassy community*

Click on Foreign Embassies in Washington, D.C. and you will be greeted with an alphabetical list of countries. Click on the country of your choice and find out more information. Great for a report.

◯ National Flags

http://155.187.10.12/flags/nation-flags.html

If your kids are doing reports on nations around the world, then they need this site. You can get images of flags from Argentina to Zambia, and more flags are being added on a regular basis. Another related site to consider is **http://www.adfa.oz.au/CS/ flg/index.html** titled "Flags."

Museums on the Web

◯ Metropolitan Museum of Art

http://www.metmuseum.org/

More than two million works of art reside at one of the largest art museums in the world. The collection spans more than 5000 years of world culture, from pre-history to the present.

● Franklin Institute of Science Museum

http://sln.fi.edu/tfi/welcome.html

This is the first online museum I entered and it is still one of my favorites. Here you can find lessons, science demonstrations, online exhibits, and just plain fun.

● Resources at the Smithsonian

http://www.si.edu/resource/start.htm

Click on Open, type in the URL above, and the nation's attic will be at your fingertips. Scroll down to Tours and take a Kids Guide to the Smithsonian. The Smithsonian Gem and Mineral collection is at **http://galaxy.einet.net/images/gems/gems-icons.html**.

● The San Francisco Museum of Fine Arts

http://www.thinker.org

Click on ImageBase once you get to this Web site and wait for a surprise. The San Francisco Museum is committed to putting all of its collection online. Currently 70,000 images are online, and you can find out detailed information about any work of art they own. This is an amazing collection, but be warned: You are not allowed to copy any of the images for resale or publishing.

⬤ The Louvre

http://www.paris.org/Musees/Louvre/

Maybe the most famous museum of them all. You will see exhibits change periodically. It's a busy site—so it takes awhile to access its riches—but it is worth it. Keep going back to catch up on the great masters.

⬤ The Rock and Roll Hall of Fame and Museum

http://www.rockhall.com/

The place on the Web to look at pop culture. If you are a secondary Social Studies, English, or Music teacher, find out more about the annual summer institute about using popular music in interdisciplinary learning.

Schools on the Web

There are lots of Web pages developed by elementary, middle and high school students and/or teachers. I find these sites interesting as they give me ideas for lessons, projects, or just for developing home pages.

⬤ Hot List of K–12 School Sites

http://www.gsn.org/hotlist/index.html

Click on the name of the state you want, and see all the elementary, middle, and high schools that have a Web site in that state. It's a good way to find out information about a school, find out what other people are learning, or create a keypal link with your class.

⦿ The American School Directory

http://www.asd.com/

If you want to find out information on just about any school in the United States, click on this address and follow the directions. You will be amazed at how many schools are connected to the Web.

AMERICAN SCHOOL DIRECTORY
"The Internet Gateway To All 108,000 K-12 Schools"

⦿ Web66 International WWW School Registry

http://web66.coled.umn.edu/schools.html

Many schools that are online are listed on this Web site. After your school has made up its home page, you can add it to this site, too. It's fun to see your school listed. In addition, you can browse the home pages out there for many good ideas about lessons and activities you can do with the Internet.

One Final Word

You have just been given the URLs to over a hundred Web sites that teachers have found to be some of the best on the Web. Go ahead, have some fun! Open these Web sites and click on the links and see all the places you can go. This is just the beginning—it's hard to pick only a hundred Web sites. If you see a Web site that should be added to this list, please write to me at **cotton@instruction.com** and I'll add it to our Web page at **http://www.csuchico.edu/Online_Classroom**.

The Internet is the most comprehensive collection of resources you will ever have access to, and it definitely belongs in your classroom now!

Chapter 3
Searching on the Web—Directories & Search Engines

You have worked with your browser on the Internet, you've had a chance to look at some of the Web sites listed, and you are having fun! It *is* fun! But you might be wondering how you find a particular piece of information when there is not a convenient URL to follow. Good question. That, by the way, is the topic of this chapter. You will learn how to search the Web using directories and search engines.

Remember that old saying "Give a person a fish, feed him for a day; teach a person to fish, feed him for a lifetime"? The Web sites in Chapter Two were the fish, and while those "fish" will keep you busy for quite a few days, they do not teach you how to fish. So let's learn how to "fish the Web."

The Main Ways to Find Information on the Web

The Web is vast, chaotic, jumbled, and disorganized, and each day it is growing more so. It is a pile of information that is added to randomly by thousands of people each week. Fortunately, there are several ways to help you find the information you want, just as card catalogs help you find books in libraries. There are at least three types of Web sites that function as "card catalogs" on the Internet. You can search by categories, by specific topics, or by using multiple search services. A categorical search is called a "directory" or an "index;" a specific topic search is called a "search engine;" and then there are meta-search engines that let you search several directories and engines at the same time. Meta-search engines work exactly the same as directories and search engines—they are just services that search a collection of other search devices. Most search services allow you to do both categorical and keyword searches so you need to know how to do both. Both types of searches are easy to do and both will provide you with the same type of information, but not always the same information and not always using the same strategies. If this sounds confusing, think about your phone book and its two sections: the white pages and the yellow pages. In the white pages you find specific information about people. In the yellow pages you find categorical information about types of businesses. Yet from both, you find out phone numbers and addresses. A search engine is similar to the white pages in the phone book, and a search directory is like the yellow pages. As with the phone book, each has their use and each are needed at various times.

Search services exist on the Web as full-fledged Web sites. They have URLs like every other Web site listed in this book. You can get to a directory or search engine in the same way you get to any Web site. Click on Open or the Open File icon in your browser, type in the URL, and hit enter. That's the easy part.

I think the best way to learn about search tools is to study one directory and one search engine so you can see for yourself. (Remember, most search tools will allow you to do both a directory/categorical search as well as a specific/keyword search.) The directory I have chosen is Yahoo at URL **http://www.yahoo.com/** and the search engine I have chosen is AltaVista at URL **http://**

www.altavista.com/. I chose Yahoo because it is the largest, oldest and most-used directory on the Internet. I chose the AltaVista search engine because it returns a lot of information in an easy-to-read format. I believe they are good examples of each type of search tool. Both of these sites are commercial ventures, so you will see advertising. In fact advertising is what pays for their development.

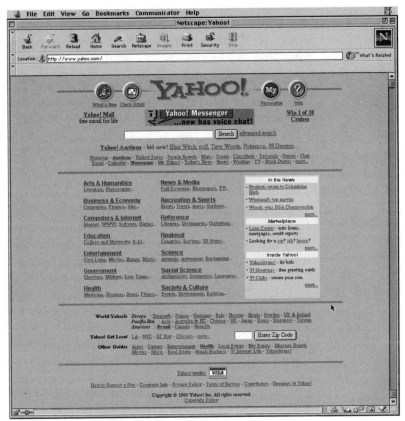

The Yahoo Web page has some cute graphics that link to "What's New," "Check E-Mail," "Personalize," and "Help." Then comes the advertisement, as this is a commercial Web site. Below that is a box with a search button next to it, and under that are a list of links to other Yahoo features: Shopping, Yellow Pages, People Search, Maps, Travel Agent, Classified, Personals, Games, Chat, E-mail, Calendar, Pager, My Yahoo, Today's News, Sports, Weather, TV, Stock Quotes, and more. If you click on any of these words or buttons, you will be transported to those sections of the

Yahoo Directory. (If you are working on a map unit, click on Maps and be surprised at what it has to offer. The same is true for weather or stock quotes.) The screen then becomes divided into two columns of words, called categories. In each category there are subcategories. There are fourteen major categories of information. Yahoo has hired a cadre of folks called "surfers" who have the job of reading Web sites, evaluating them according to Yahoo standards, and then categorizing them correctly. If a Web site doesn't fit in one of the categories, it's not included in the Yahoo database. Therefore, the database is limited by the number of Web sites that can be read and evaluated in a finite amount of time.

Let's try looking up dinosaurs, as they seem to be a big topic in many elementary schools. Scroll to Science, as dinosaurs are probably in that category. Click on it and another screen appears. Click on "animals, insects and pets," which will take you to another screen where "dinosaurs" is listed. Click on that link and you will see a "mess" of dinosaur related Web sites that Yahoo has screened into its database.

Let's try this again. Say you are seeking information about Frank Lloyd Wright. You know he was an architect, so you click on the Arts and Humanities category. When the next screen appears, look for a category that fits best. In this case it is "Design Arts." The number in parentheses after the category is the number of Web sites that Yahoo has in its database on that topic. Click on Design Arts and the next screen has a category for Architects. Click on it. This will bring you to another screen where you can narrow down your selection some more. Here there is a link to "masters." Since Frank Lloyd Wright was a great architect, this might be a good selection. Scroll down the page of masters and you will see a link to Frank Lloyd Wright near the bottom of the list. It too has a number after it. Click on that link and you find yet another page devoted to Frank Lloyd Wright and some of his masterpieces. Each link that has a number after it indicates that more screens of information are available. Links that end with an "@" indicate that the heading is listed in multiple places within the Yahoo hierarchy. If you click on that link, it will take you to a different subcategory within Yahoo.

If you use the categorical search as described above, you need to have some background knowledge on the subject and you have to use logical deduction. It also takes some time, because you have to think of broad categories and narrow them down to pinpoint your topic over a series of several different screens. If you do not have the background information, you can sidestep the categories by typing in a search query on the Yahoo home page. Type "Frank Lloyd Wright" on the search line of the Yahoo home page. Click Search and another screen appears with five boxes that are labeled Categories, Web Sites, Web Pages, Related News, and Net Events. If you click on Categories and Web Sites you will see pages that have been screened into the Yahoo database. If you click on Web Pages, Related News, and Net Events, you will find information that has been collected by Yahoo, but not screened into their categorical system. Therefore, with Yahoo you have the choice of searching both the Web or the smaller Yahoo database.

Unlike Yahoo, the folks at AltaVista do not physically look at each Web site. They use a "bot," which is short for robot, that collects

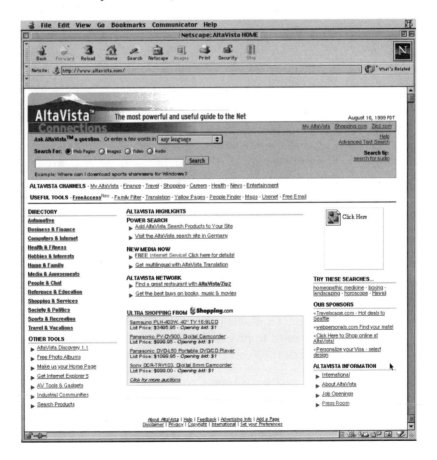

Web sites and stores them on a large database. When you search for a word or phrase, the bot "finds" that word or phrase from the database. The AltaVista bot has also developed categories to make searching easier.

To use AltaVista, go to **http://www.altavista.com** and type in your query or keyword in the search box that says "Ask AltaVista a question or enter a few words in (language—state the language you prefer)." AltaVista will respond by giving you a list of all the Web pages in their index that relate to your topic. The most relevant content will appear at the top of the results list. You will get a lot of information back. After you have received a long list of potential URLs, you can narrow them down by clicking the advanced button.

Let's try the two searches we did in Yahoo to compare and contrast a directory with a search engine. Using the AltaVista search engine, type in "dinosaur." A new screen appears that has two sections: A gold-colored box that says "Related Searches," and (after an advertisement) a line that says AltaVista found almost 400,000 possible hits. Click on an item in the Related Searches box and see what happens. Then hit the back button and scroll down the list of hits.

Now let's redo the search for Frank Lloyd Wright. Type in "Frank Lloyd Wright," and you will get over 23,000 possible hits. At this point you can scroll down to the Related Searches box and see if there are any useful links, or you can scroll farther down and see many more links. Click on the links that seem pertinent to your study. You can also refine your search as you did above, narrowing it down to include only the exact words you are seeking. In this case they would be "Frank," "Lloyd," and "Wright." Click on one of them and you'll probably find the information you are seeking.

For topics that naturally fall into categories, a directory search works well. For topics where you know the essential keyword, a search engine is useful. In either a directory or a search engine, you need to practice logical problem-solving, as that is what makes these such useful teaching tools.

You now have some actual practice doing a search. You've compared a directory and a search engine search. In either case, you have to use some logic, or that uncommon quality called "common sense." Also, if you look at the two sets of lists, you might notice there is some overlap. That's good. It says you are on the right track. If I don't get any overlap, I wonder if I have done the search correctly. You might want to practice some more. Search for a topic—like Stock Exchange, Volcanoes, or Native American Legends—and see what happens when you use both search methods. If you want something more challenging, search for an issue like School Reform.

Now try the same two searches using a Meta-search engine. InferenceFind, at **http://www.infind.com/** is considered one of the best meta-search engines out there by Search IQ (**http://www.searchiq.com**). InferenceFind uses information from six search engines in parallel format, which means it "calls them up at the same time." It then merges the results, removes redundancies and groups the results in a logical format. Dogpile, at **http://www.dogpile.com/** uses twenty-five different search engines and directories to find links to your query. Profusion, at **http://www.profusion.com/** also uses several search engines, however you can choose the best three, the three fastest, all of them, or any one of them. These are just a few of the many meta-search tools out there.

What to Use

The things I look for in a search service for school are speed, safety and accuracy. I'm not the most patient person in the world, so I like the speedier search services better than the sluggish ones. However, some of the speediest ones also produce a lot of information that is not pertinent to my search. Search engines look for matches to a keyword. When we typed "Frank Lloyd Wright," there were 23,000+ hits. I am led to wonder if there are really that many pieces of information on Frank Lloyd Wright out there. If you look at some of the Web sites, you will find that they have information about folks who are of the Frank Lloyd Wright school of architecture, or folks who happen to have "frank" written on their Web site. This leads to a discussion of the "noise-to-hit ratio," and some search engines are "noisier" than others. Noise is a "bad hit," or a link to something that does not relate to your search query. The "noise-to-hit ratio" depends on how the search engines collect their databases. Some search engines have a database collection that only includes words found in the "headers" and "titles" of a Web page. These are narrow databases and produce a high-hit, low-noise ratio. Other search engines collect the first one hundred words found on a Web page. These search engines are a bit broader, but also produce a high-hit, low-noise ratio. However, the AltaVista database collects every word found on the Web page. This makes it a high-hit, high-noise search engine. It is, however, a fast search engine. You have to decide which is best. For that reason, I like to use a couple of different search engines and compare their list of hits.

Now that you've had a little taste each of a directory, a search engine, and a meta-search engine, you need to decide which is best for the type of search you are doing. Let me offer you a few advantages and disadvantages for each, then you can make the decision whether to choose the directory section or the search section.

Pros and Cons of Directories

Directories are good browsing devices. Use the categories as a tool to guide you to material you might not find any other way. They are orderly, moving from general information to specific information about a topic. Also, a directory is made by real people, who have reviewed the Web sites and have used some sort of selection process. For this reason, directories are good starting places to find out more about a topic. However, if you are looking for U.S. History, do you search in Art and Humanities, or Social Science? Both categories are present, and history can fit in either one of them. (Yahoo puts history in Social Science, by the way.) I especially like to use directories at schools, because they help reinforce deductive reasoning.

There are, however, disadvantages to them. If you don't know the category to start with, you might never find your information. If you can't figure out a specific category, then use the search mode provided. Another disadvantage is the size limit of the database. Since people have to read and categorize Web sites, some URLs might be excluded because they have not been reviewed yet. New URLs are constantly being added to the Internet and it is next to impossible for reviewers to screen, categorize and cross-reference every URL on a daily basis.

Pros and Cons for Search Engines

When you know a keyword or phrase, or a specific name for what you are looking for, a search engine is an efficient way to find information. In the Frank Lloyd Wright search, we were led directly to a list that in the end could contain 23,000+ hits. That's impressive. You have many choices, and some are bound to be relevant. You just have to wade through them.

However, there is a drawback. You need to know a keyword or phrase, and you have to be willing to go through many links that might not be relevant to your needs.

Take your pick: directories for categorical searches, search engines for keyword searches. Depending on your needs, both can provide you with lots of information.

To add more fodder to your information overload, also consider a meta-search engine. They are fast, they tend to be accurate, and many *do* remove redundancies. I believe that the meta-search engine is part of the future of the net. However, to make it work, keyword search engines and directories are necessary.

Other Web Sites for Searching the Internet

There are many different search devices on the Internet. If you are using Netscape, click on NetSearch and you will see the impressive list that the Netscape Corporation has developed. If you are using Internet Explorer, click on search and you can program your favorite search engine to use time and again. There is actually a Web site devoted to search tools. Go to Beaucoup at **http://www.beaucoup.com** and you will see a list of over 2500 search engines and directories. If you want to play on this Web site, you might never return to reality. In addition, go to Search IQ at **http://www.searchiq.com**. This Web site rates search services according to an IQ score. It has a great tutorial and guide feature, as well as a direct link to many other search services.

As befits the name of this book, *The Online Classroom: Teaching with the Internet*, after you have learned how to find information on the Web, you need to teach those strategies to your students. Maybe you've noticed that some of the Web sites you have seen are not appropriate for kids. As much as I'm an advocate of using online technology in classrooms, I know that there are "bad things" out there on the net. In "netspeak," you want your students to find information on the Web safely. You therefore want child-safe Web sites. The best way to find child-safe Web sites is by using child-safe search tools. They exist!

There are a several search tools that have been developed with children and your family in mind. Some of these search tools screen URLs for X-rated or inappropriate Web sites. The databases on these services are smaller, and therefore they will limit your search. They are useful for children and for you. When I'm looking for good Web sites for kids, I use these more restricted search tools first and branch out from there. You might want to check out these search tools to use in your class.

Safe Search Tools for Kids

Yahooligans! (**http://www.yahooligans.com**) is a child-safe version of Yahoo. It looks similar to Yahoo, but instead of fourteen categories, it has ten. This Web directory is aimed for children between seven and twelve years old. Most of the Web sites listed on Yahooligans have been submitted by people who believe they are accessible, accurate, appropriate and appealing for children.

KidsClick! (**http://sunsite.berkeley.edu/KidsClick!**) is a Web directory that has been developed by librarians. The KidsClick! database has about 1500 Web sites that are categorized to fit school curricula. KidsClick! has one other quality: the Web sites all have a reading level assigned to them. What this means is the Web sites are not only child-safe, but the kids will be able to read them too.

Ask Jeeves for Kids (**http://www.ajkids.com**) is made to answer the questions that kids always seem to ask. Like the "adult" version of Ask Jeeves (**http://www.jeeves.com**), instead of typing in a keyword, you ask a question and the search engine will try to answer it. Sometimes it will respond with more questions to narrow down the answer. AJKids states that the hits they recommend are G-rated.

The EdView SMART Search for Kids at **http://school.edview.com/search/** has a database organized for elementary, middle, and high school level kids. The folks at EdView screen Web sites for content, credibility, and design with the idea that the information will be safe for kids. It works much the same as the Yahoo or Yahooligans directories.

While the search tools above are made expressly for children, some search tools have created a way to filter or block Web sites. For these search tools, you will have to click a button to turn on a filter. Of course, this means that your students can easily click on the button and turn it off.

Magellan at **http://magellan.excite.com/** has a feature called "Green Light Sites." These sites are located only on the Web (not **ftp://** or **gopher://**), and this feature applies only to the selected Web site, not to outside links. If you use the Green Light Sites option, you get a targeted search list of reviewed sites that, at the time of review, contained no content intended for mature audiences.

The GO Network has a couple of search tools: Lycos (**http://www.go.com/**) and Infoseek (**http://infoseek.go.com/**). Each uses GOguardian, which is similar to Green Light Sites in Magellan. You can click GOguardian on or off, which means your students can also click it on or off. It filters out inappropriate adult content, so you can feel more comfortable about having young people explore the Web. When I asked a group of teachers to check out GOguardian by asking them to search for X-rated words with the GOguardian on and off, they determined that it did work!

AltaVista has the AV Family Filter, which can also be turned on and off, but with the added advantage of a password. If you require a password, then Family Filter cannot be turned off until the correct password has been typed. Like GOguardian, it seems to filter out X-rated and other objectionable Web sites.

What to Use when Searching the Web

For elementary school lessons, I like to use KidsClick and Yahooligans. For middle school and high school, I like to use Yahoo, InfoSeek and AltaVista. For home, I use Yahoo, AltaVista, and InferenceFind. I also use Boolean search strategies to narrow down more complicated searches.

Boolean Searches

There's at least one more thing to know: How to do a Boolean search. Some, not all, of the search tools listed will let you do Boolean keyword searches. I remember the first time I heard the word Boolean. It was during my MA stats class, and I dreaded the thought of the whole thing. Well, seeing it on a search tool started the old fear again. Don't let it happen to you! I finally have Boolean searches down cold! And they are not even hard. Just put it down as one more thing you have to know to do a good search— and it's one more thing you can teach your kids. They'll thank you for it later.

Boolean searches rely on "words" called operators: and, or, not, near, adjacent, " . . . " and (. . .). That's all. If you open WebCrawler (**http://Webcrawler.com**) and click on Advanced or go directly to **http://www.Webcrawler.com/WebCrawler/Help/ Advanced.html**, you will see a clear explanation of each of these operators. I'll paraphrase the WebCrawler explanation for you here. Say I want to find Web sites about the History of China. If the search tool I am using requires Boolean operators, then I have the choices listed on the next page:

Operator	Example	What you'll get back	Result
AND	China AND History	Web sites that include both of the words—e.g. Web sites with both China AND History	AND will limit your search
OR	China OR History	Web sites that include either of the words or both—e.g. sites with China OR those with History OR those with both China and History.	OR will broaden your search
NOT	China NOT Pottery	Web sites that include the first word or phrase but not the second—e.g. sites with China NOT pottery (the dishes).	NOT will limit your search
"..." (quotation marks)	"Chinese History"	Web sites that include the phrase as it is written	"..." will limit your search
NEAR	China NEAR 25 History	Web sites that have China and History written within 25 words of each other	NEAR will limit your search
ADJ (adjacent)	China ADJ History	Web sites that have the two words written next to each other i.e., China History	ADJ will limit your search
(...)	China NOT (pottery OR porcelain)	Web sites containing the first word but not the others	(...) will limit your search

Boolean searches should be easy, but as usual, there is a fly in the ointment. Some search tools, like WebCrawler, use "or" as the default operator; other search tools use "and" as the default operator. Some don't use either. Then there is just one more little problem. Not all of them use the same Boolean symbols. Some use colons (:) and commas (,) where others use +, - and \. When you are not sure what operators a particular search tool uses, read the help section on the home page of the search tool, or look for a link that indicates how you can improve your search results. Most search tools have a built-in Help function or a Frequently Asked

Ten Search Tips for Classroom Teachers

1. Many Web directories and key word search engines have a "help" or "advanced" button. Click on it for more detailed directions on how to use that search tool.

2. Practice using the search tool on topics you know something about before you go on a "real search." That way you can learn something about the logic that is being used.

3. Use a Web directory like Yahoo (www.yahoo.com), or Yahooligans! (www.yahooligans.com), or KidsClick! (sunsite.berkeley.edu/kidsclick) before using a search engine. Examine the titles of hits from a Web directory to discover related topics before doing a keyword search.

4. When starting a search, brainstorm related words first. If you are looking for the music from *West Side Story*, search for *West Side Story* instead of music or musical.

5. Plural words generate too much information—hits are more specific with singular words, as there is no "s" to confuse the finding tool.

6. When typing in a keyword-query, remember that lower case letters will broaden a search; UPPER CASE LETTERS WILL NARROW A SEARCH; Upper and lower case will create a more specific search pattern.

7. When you don't know how to spell something, use a wildcard (usually *). If you don't know how to spell musician, search for music* and your search engine will look for Web sites that have any form of "music" in them, such as "musical" "musicals" and "musician."

8. When collecting Web sites for a unit of instruction, try screened search tools first, then broaden out to more general search tools.

9. Learn one search tool before branching out to another. Then use only two or three search tools and use them well.

10. Both Web directories and search engines are needed to get a better sampling of information.

Questions (FAQ) section that will give you information about how to develop a "good search." If the search tool uses a Boolean search pattern, follow the directions and use the correct operators for that search tool. When you know the right words to use for each tool, you will be rewarded with better results.

Scavenger Hunt, Anyone?

You now have had a good introduction to search tools found on the Web. There is still a lot more to learn, but this is enough for now. You know that directories are categorical, and search engines rely on keywords. You know that there are few pure directories or search engines, as most search devices offer both types of searches. You know a little bit about Boolean searches, and you have URLs for several search tools that are good for both school and home. From what you have just learned, choose a directory and a search engine from the list and see if you can find the following items. This exercise is something you might want to do with your kids, too. It helps teach logic skills, as well as develop a sense of how things are organized on the Web, and how interconnected they all are.

The rationale for this type of lesson is simple. If you are going to be using the Internet, you need to know how to gain access to information. Just like guide words are necessary for learning how to use a phone book or dictionary, directories and search engines are necessary to learn how to find information on the Internet.

The procedure is easy. Introduce your students to a directory and a search engine. Tell them about Boolean operators. Walk them through a couple of examples. Then give them a list of things they have to find. Evaluation is almost self-explanatory. If they find Web sites that match the hunt items, they are successful. At the end of this chapter is a middle-grades level worksheet I have used. You can copy it or you make up your own scavenger hunt. The answers are below.

Scavenger Hunt Answers:

1. 92. I used InfoSeek and typed in "Periodic Table of Elements," and followed a link to MIT. See **http://www-tech.mit.edu/Chemicool/** for more information. I used InferenceFind and typed in "atomic number and uranium" and followed a link in the United Kingdom. See **http://www.shef.ac.uk/chemistry/Web-elements/index.html**.

2. 4808 Hollywood Blvd., Los Angeles, CA. I used Yahoo and typed in "Hollyhock House" which led me to **http://www.fohh.org/**. After scanning the index I found the address.

3. False. Robinson Crusoe was written in 1719. And Alice in Wonderland was written in 1865. I used AltaVista and made two queries: "Defoe and Robinson Crusoe" and "Carroll and Alice in Wonderland." See **http://www.incompetech.com/authors/defoe/** and **http://aj.encyclopedia.com/articles/02345.html** for more information. By the way, some sources say Crusoe was written in 1719, others say 1721.

4. Hafa Adai. I used Yahoo to search for Guam, then followed the links for language. See **http://www.gov.gu/index.html**. I also used InferenceFind, and queried "chamorro and guam" and was led to the same Web site.

5. William A. Wheeler. I cheated. I knew that the White House home page (**http://www.whitehouse.gov**) had a listing of presidents, so I went there first, and found the

Web site for President Hayes at **http://
www.whitehouse.gov/WH/glimpse/presidents/html/rh19-
plain.html**. This did not tell me who was his Vice President. Next I went to WebCrawler and typed in "Rutherford
B. Hayes," clicked on the link to the Internet Public Library. *Voilà*, I found the answer.

You can make a Scavenger Hunt as easy, or hard, as you wish.
You can search for answers that jump out at you, or for embedded
answers that your kids will have to read a bit before they know
they are on the right track. You can develop hunts for people,
places, and things on the Web as easily as you can develop hunts
for ideas, facts, and opinions. You can develop hunts to introduce
a topic to your students, or you can develop hunts that offer them
practice with logic in several different topics. I also let kids make
their own scavenger hunts. One small group develops a hunt and
another group tries to find the URLs.

Don't forget to look at the skills your kids are using and learning.
They are learning how to skim and scan a Web site for information that reinforces their reading skills. They are learning how to
sort and categorize information, use higher-order thinking skills,
reinforce writing and typing skills, and the list goes on. As you
can see, the Internet is a teaching tool.

I hope you had fun learning how to search the Internet. I hate to
tell you this, but we have just skimmed the surface of searching
the Net. But this is enough for now. I really hope you develop a
couple of scavenger hunts for your kids to do. If you have a super
successful one, e-mail it to me and I'll include it on the Web site
for this book (**http://www.csuchico.edu/Online_Classroom**). You
can always reach me at **cotton@instruction.com**. I'm looking
forward to hearing from you soon!

Scavenger Hunt

Name: _____ Date: _____

1. What is the atomic number of uranium?

The answer: _____

URL where you found the answer: _____

2. Where is Hollyhock House located?

The answer: _____

URL where you found the answer: _____

3. True or False: *Robinson Crusoe* **(by Daniel Defoe) and** *Alice in Wonderland* **(by Lewis Carroll) were written in the same year? (Please indicate the year.)**

The answer: _____

URL where you found the answer: _____

4. If you want to say "hello" to Chamorro-speaking folks on Guam, what is one word or phrase you would use?

The answer: _____

URL where you found the answer: _____

5. Who was Vice President when Rutherford B. Hayes President of the United States?

The answer: _____

URL where you found the answer: _____

Chapter 4
Developing and Designing a Web Site

Now that you've seen many Web pages, you are probably thinking you might want to make one up on your own. You can! In fact, you and your students can learn to use HTML (HyperText Mark-up Language) so that you can develop and publish a Web site for your school or class. It's not really a programming language, it is just a set of typesetting style codes, so don't let that scare you away. It's easy, and some would say fun!

As with anything that deals with technology, there are at least three ways to learn HTML coding. There are HTML editors that allow you to create and manage Web pages exactly as they are viewed on the Web. There are HTML converters that take a document and convert it to HTML, and there is the "old fashioned" method of writing the HTML code. Each method will lead to a Web page. If you like to see how something works, then the "old fashioned" method works best. If you want to see a product now, then use a converter. If you want to see a product now and still have some control over the design, then use an editor. When I teach HTML to kids or teachers, I've found that when folks learn the basics of HTML coding first (i.e., the old fashioned method), they can use a HTML editor more efficiently. Think of how you learn best, then select the procedure that's best for you.

The Basic HTML Code

To create your own Web page, you need a list of the HTML codes and any text editor. I like to use "Simple Text" on my Mac or "Notepad" on my PC, which are programs that are available in either MacOS or Windows 95/98. You can also use any word processor, as long as you save the document as an ASCII file or a text file.

HTML uses codes called tags, which are just letters, words, numbers or phrases that tell your Web browser how to display a Web page. The tags are placed outside of the text of a document to format the page and to mark where pictures, graphics, other links, type sizes, colors, or fonts should be placed on the browser screen. Here's a sample of HTML code: **\<H1\>**The Online Classroom**\</H1\>**. If you type that code using your word processor, save it to a text file named "toc.html," and open the file on Netscape or Internet Explorer, you will see:

The Online Classroom

written in large type.

I think of HTML as primarily a bookend code. If you want your books to stand up on the shelf, you need a bookend at the left and right ends of the row of books. The same idea follows with HTML: You need a tag at the beginning and end of every string of text. Angled brackets **\< \>** at the beginning say, "Code starts here." Angled brackets with a forward slash **\</ \>** says, "Code ends here." For example, the tag **\<B\>** causes text to be written in bold letters. "B" for "bold" inside the angled brackets indicates an HTML coded command: "This is a code command: Turn on B for Bold!" When you get to the end of the word or phrase, you key in **\</B\>** which tells the machine: "This is a code command: Turn off B for Bold!" Try it. Type the same phrase as above, but make it bold: **\<H1\>\<B\>**The Online Classroom**\</B\>\</H1\>** and see what happens. It should look like this:

The Online Classroom.

HTML consists of many such tags: tags for headlines, tags for underlining, tags for italics, tags for titles, and tags for paragraph breaks. But don't be overwhelmed by all the tags! Many of the tags are alliterative, such as "B for bold" or "I for italics." After you've coded your first few Web pages, you will soon remember most of the commonly used tags. Netscape Navigator and Internet Explorer also support tags that allow you to set up tables, customize backgrounds, or add color and graphics. But the problem with HTML is that it is a simple formatting language— not too complex. If you're accustomed to setting type and using complex desktop publishing programs, you will find HTML, and its quite limited range of typographic possibilities, rather clunky.

One of the best ways to start setting up a home page is to consult the many online pages developed as teaching tools for folks like you. Search Yahoo for "HTML" and you will find hundreds of Web sites out there; many of them are very helpful. You can also buy an HTML guidebook in a bookstore (in fact, you can order one online from Amazon.com or Barnes and Noble (**http:// www.barnesandnoble.com/**), or borrow one from the library. Just be sure you get a recent edition, as HTML changes and grows every year. Listed below are a few beginning HTML sites you might want to visit.

HTML Web Sites to visit

Lissa's HTML Help for Kids at **http://members.aol.com/ xolissaxo/index.htmlhelp.html** is written by a twelve-year-old who knows HTML, and has written some commercial pages. This is a simple straightforward delivery of the topic.

The HTML Interactive Tutorial for Beginners at **http:// davesite.com/webstation/html/** is a good place to start too. Dave Kristula updates the Web site regularly, so it supports the latest version of HTML. The tutorial can be printed out so you can refer to it time and again.

123 . . . Easy at **http://spring-board.com/123easy/map.html** is one of my favorite starting places to teach HTML. It consists of five easy pages of information about coding, graphics, backgrounds, pictures, forms, and more.

The Mechanical Monkey at **http://dspace.dial.pipex.com/leuhusen/index.shtml** has tutorials, design tips, and original art that you can use for free.

The BareBones Guide to HTML at **http://www.werbach.com/barebones/** leads you to a Web site where you can download a good guidebook. This is especially good for folks who need to see hardcopy in order to truly digest the information.

The Web Designer at **http://web.canlink.com/webdesign/** has a "help desk" feature. Click on the HTML tag you want to know more about and you will find a short, clear description of what you need to do.

To see what a Web page looks like without the window dressing—that is, in "bare" HTML—you can tell your browser to show you the document source code. In Netscape, go to View in the pull-down menu and scroll down until you see Document Source and click on it. For Internet Explorer, go to View and scroll down to Source. In the PC environment you will immediately see both the tags and text that were used to make that Web page look as it does. In the Mac environment, your browser may launch an external program to show you the codes. In any case, you will see lines of text that start and end with <bracketed letters, words and numbers>, and in between is something that looks like English. These <bracketed words> are the tags that have been "embedded" into the text; they are not seen when the page is displayed normally.

If you have already coded a home page, the tags and text you see will have meaning to you. However, if you have only looked at browser screens and never delved any deeper into the medium, reading tags is like reading a foreign language. But don't let the techie jargon scare you into thinking that you cannot design and develop your own home page! If you have walked the Web only a little bit—especially in regions where educators roam—you will have seen Web pages written by elementary-school kids. If kids can do it, you can do it! You do not need to be a computer programmer to develop a Web page; you only need to know what you want your Web page to say, time to hunt and peck, and patience.

HTML Basics

The Web page or document you want to code has four sections: Document Type, Header, Title, and Body. The document type is **<HTML>** and is placed at the beginning of the document or file. At the very end of the document or file, you write **</HTML>** as a finishing touch. The first and last bookend.

The Title is the name of the document as it is going to show up on the top center of the browser window, right after it says Netscape or Internet Explorer. It is written **<TITLE>** and at the end of the title, **</TITLE>**. The header **<HEAD>** is the area in the document where the title is placed, and it ends with **</HEAD>**. Lastly comes the Body of the file or document, the bulk of the page. It is coded **<BODY>** and **</BODY>**.

Here's an example:

```
<HTML>
<HEAD>
<TITLE>What's It All About, Anyway?</TITLE>
</HEAD>
<BODY>your stuff goes here</BODY>
</HTML>
```

HTML is not case sensitive. However, it is recommended that you use upper case letters. What you must not do is forget the **<brackets>** or / marks. If even one **>** mark is left off, the tag will not be read correctly, and the document will not appear as you want it to appear. Remember, though, that URLs are case-sensitive. Using a capital letter instead of a lowercase letter can break a link.

You have noticed that most Web sites have a background image or color. You can add those to the code. For a background image type

<BODY BACKGROUND="name-of-background.jpg">

between **</HEAD>** and **<BODY>**.

A good list of background images can be found at **http://dspace.dial.pipex.com/leuhusen/bkgrnds.htm**. If you find a background image that you like, copy it to a file on your hard drive and then you can use it.

For a plain background color,

<BODY BGCOLOR="#000000" (whatever color # you want)**>**

There are many good color charts around, but I like the one at Bluemoon at **http://www.freeyellow.com/members5/ bluemoon770/page3.html**.

Sample HTML

The phrase "The Information Superhighway" is coded several different ways below. Look at the tags, and see how the printed result changes.

Command	Coding	Result
Bold	**<B>**The Information Superhighway**</B>**	**The Information Superhighway**
Italics	**<I>**The Information Superhighway**</I>**	*The Information Superhighway*
Bold, Italics (together)	**<I><B>**The Information Superhighway**</B></I>**	***The Information Superhighway***
Centered	**<CENTER>**The Information Superhighway**</CENTER>**	The Information Superhighway

If you get the general idea, then you are ready for some more complicated coding. Use **
** (line break) at the end of a line when you want a single carriage return. Use **<HR>** to put in a horizontal rule, or line, across a document. These are two tags, or codes, that do not need the **</>** tag or the other bookend. To write a paragraph start with **<P>** and end with **</P>** for a double carriage return. Some examples follow on the next page.

Code	What You Write	Result
Line break or single carriage return	She likes to sing.**\ ** He likes to dance.**\ **	She likes to sing. He likes to dance.
Double carriage return or paragraph	**\<P>**She likes to sing.**\</P>** Helikes to dance.**\</P>**	She likes to sing. He likes to dance.
Horizontal Rule	**\<HR>**	————————————

To make lists, use either **\<UL>\</UL>** (unordered list) or **\<OL>\</OL>** (ordered list) tags along with **\<LI>** (link) tag. An Unordered list is not numbered, while an ordered list is numbered 1, 2, 3, etc. Here's an example using the **\<HR>**, **\
, **\<UL> and **\<P>** tags:

HTML Code

\<HR>\<P>
We saw these animals:
\<P>
\<UL>
\<LI>goats
\<LI>pigs
\<LI>cows
\</UL>\<HR>

What appears on the browser window

———————————————

We saw these animals:

- goats
- pigs
- cows

———————————————

Here's the same example using a numbered list:

HTML Code	What appears on the browser window
<HR><P>	————————————
We saw these animals:**</P>**	We saw these animals:
<OL>	1. goats
<LI>goats	2. pigs
<LI>pigs	3. cows
<LI>cows	
</OL>	————————————
<HR>	

There's more. You want to connect your page to other pages, so you need to create hypertext links. Those are the underlined/colored words you see on Web pages that allow you to bounce from one page to another. There is a specific coding for them, too. Every time you want to create a link, you must anchor it in the main body of the text. Since "anchor" starts with "A" the tag starts out with a "**<A HREF=**" and a twist. Next, you want to refer to the other Web site. All Web sites are identified by Uniform Resource Locators, so you type in the URL. Here is a sample that will take a visitor to the Smithsonian Institution:

<P><A HREF="http://www.si.edu/start.htm">The Smithsonian Institution</A></P>

If you typed this in on a HTML document, it would look something like the following on a browser screen (you'll have to imagine that it is in blue type):

<u>The Smithsonian Institution</u>

and, by clicking on the underlined phrase, your visitor will be viewing the home page for the Smithsonian Institution in Washington, D.C. The hypertext link is relatively easy to remember if you know what the various parts represent. The chart below explains what they mean.

HTML Code	**What it means**
<P>	New paragraph
<A	The opening anchor.
HREF=	The hypertext reference.
"http://www.si.edu/resource/start.htm"	The URL for the new document. (Don't forget the quotation marks at the beginning and end of the URL.)
>	End of the opening anchor
Smithsonian Institution	Underlined hypertext link the browser screen will show.
</A>	Ending anchor.
</P>	End of paragraph, double carriage return.

The code to insert images in your pages is similar to the code that commands a link to be inserted. Online images are not actually part of the HTML file, but are links to separate image files. Instead of inserting a document that has **.html** at the end of the URL, it will have the abbreviation for the type of graphics file it is. Some of these abbreviations are **.gif**, **.jpg**, **.mpg**. Almost all Web browsers will have image reading programs that support the types of image files mentioned above. So, if you are going to put in an image, you will write the following tag:

> **<img src="egc.gif">**

Can you decode that tag?

HTML Code   What it means

HTML Code	**What it means**
<img src=	The opening tag telling the browser to view an image
"egc.gif"	title of the image file
>	end of the tag

Notice that the URL used in the previous example is very short and does not begin with **http://**. This is called "relative addressing" and it only works if the files are in the same folder as the Web site.

Letters and Fonts

The six type sizes available HTML, range from <H1>, the largest, to <H6>, the smallest:

HTML Code	What appears in the browser window
<H1>MAIN TITLE**</H1>**	# MAIN TITLE
<H2>SMALL TITLE**</H2>**	## SMALL TITLE
<H3>SUB-HEAD**</H3>**	### SUB-HEAD
<H4>SUB-SUB-HEAD**</H4>**	SUB-SUB-HEAD
<H5>SUB-SUB-SUB-HEAD**</H5>**	SUB-SUB-SUB-HEAD
<H6>THE SMALL PRINT**</H6>**	THE SMALL PRINT

Be forewarned that some browsers cannot read **<H5>** or **<H6>** because they are too small. Netscape and Internet Explorer, however, can read them.

You can also change the font type this way:

<BODY BGCOLOR=....>
<FONT FACE="....">

(Write the body of the document)
</FONT>

You need to select a font that most folks have on their computers such as Arial, Helvetica, Times New Roman, etc.

As a helper, keep this reference chart handy, or if you want to find an even bigger reference page, go visit the folks at WebMonkey, a page sponsored by HotWired at **http://www.hotwired.com/webmonkey/reference/index.html** and print out a very complete list of tags and styles.

Style	Mnemonic	Code
Bold	Bold	**\<B>\</B>**
Italics	Italics	**\<I>\</I>**
Underline	Underline	**\<U>\</U>**
Large Print	1	**\<H1>\</H1>**
Small Print	6	**\<H6>\</H6>**
Center	Center	**\<CENTER>\</CENTER>**
Unordered list	list without numbers	**\<UL> \</UL>** (**\<LI>** needed in front of each item)
Ordered list	list with numbers	**\<OL> \</OL>** (**\<LI>** needed in front of each item)

What follows is a template for a pretty basic Web page:

```
<HTML>
<HEAD>
<TITLE><CENTER> Title Of Page </CENTER></TITLE>
</HEAD>
<BODY BACKGROUND="name-of-bg.jpg" TEXT="#000000"
BGCOLOR="#ffffff">
<HR>
——Your stuff goes here——
<HR>
</BODY>
</HTML>
```

HTML Editors, Converters and Generators

Remember, I said there were several ways you could learn HTML. What has just been described is hand coding or the "old fashioned" method. I think it is fun and interesting, but it can get tedious. That's why there are helpers out there to make it easier. I've found however, that the helpers are very difficult to use when you don't know the basic coding guidelines.

You might remember that I teach an online class based on this book, from Indiana University. My students (who are mostly teachers) are required to design a Web page for the class. About half decide to "code" on their own, while the other half use an editor program. It's really up to you and what you are comfortable with learning. On the other hand, when I teach HTML coding to school kids, I always teach them the code and the process long before I introduce an editor program. It seems to make the editor program make more sense that way.

There are many HTML editors on the Web that you can download as freeware (it's free), shareware (you pay a nominal amount) or CareWare (no money, just care for the Planet and the people and each other). There is WebWizard: The Duke of URL at **http://www.halcyon.com/artamedia/webwizard/**, a freeware program. Arachnophilia at **http://www.arachnoid.com/** is a CareWare program that many of my teachers use and recommend.

If you want to use a more formal HTML editor you can buy them. For a preview of Adobe PageMill, go to **http://www.adobe.com/prodindex/pagemill/main.html** and you can download a free trial copy of Adobe PageMill (15 days for Windows, 30 days for Macs). You can view information about Claris Home Page at **http://www.filemaker.com/products/homepage3.html**.

There are also "free" HTML editors on your computer right now, if you know where to look for them. If you are using one of the recent versions of Microsoft Word, you can save documents as HTML documents. (Use the "save as" command and where it says "save as file type" open the box and scroll to HTML document.) In addition, the most recent version of Microsoft Office has an HTML editor program called FrontPage. If you are using version

4.x or higher of Internet Explorer for Windows, you have FrontPage Express built into the browser. If you are using Netscape Navigator 4.x or higher, you have Composer built in the browser, which is another HTML editor program. In Netscape Navigator, go to the pull-down menus, click on Communicator, then scroll to Composer. You are now in an HTML editor program. You might have one or more of these HTML editors available, but you might not know how to use them. That's when knowing the HTML code comes in handy.

When all else fails, you can go to the Web to get your Web site coded for you. The Hayi Homepage Generator is on the Web for you to create your own homepage without knowing anything about HTML. Just follow the options, select the ones you like, and a Web page will be generated for you. It is located at **http://www.lafayette.edu/acs/hayi/html-form.html**.

Web Site Design

You just had the crash course of basic HTML coding. Now's the time to add some life to your Web site. I'm sure you've seen Web sites that are an ugly color, or have a busy background. And you are wondering, "Why would anybody do that to it?" I've wondered the same thing and, like my mother used to say, "Beauty is in the eye of the beholder." What is beautiful to you may not be beautiful to someone else. (Also realize that backgrounds and other elements of Web design display differently on different platforms, browsers, and computer monitors. Check your Web work on a friend's computer to see if it looks like it "should.")

The first item you need before starting a Web site is a location for it! If your page cannot find a home, then you don't have a page. Many schools have space on their server for your Web site. However, if that is not the case, check with your local Internet provider, as many of them offer between one and five MB of space for a personal Web page. Angelfire at **http://www.angelfire.com/** has free pages, as do Geocities (**http://www.geocities.com/join/**) and Xoom (**http://xoom.com/webspace/**). To find more free pages, use your favorite search service and query "free page."

A good Web site starts with the home or index page. It should have all the important information seen on the first screen without any scrolling. When you open a home page and see nothing and you have to wait for a big graphic to appear, you're probably going to open another site as soon as possible. For this reason, you want to capture your reader's attention quickly with information that can be seen at a glance.

A good Web site should not be too busy. Don't go overboard with color and graphics and different font sizes. While variety might be the spice of life, it can be distracting and is another way to discourage people from visiting your Web site. After all, if you are creating an information bank for your students, you want them to visit your Web site, stay there, learn something, then come back again and again.

Look at some professionally-made Web sites. See what they have done regarding color, font, and logo, and take your cues from them. Usually, the logo is moderately small, the colors are appealing to the eye, and you see an index or other means of telling you the content of the Web site, so you can navigate around the many pages quickly. If you have a logo, don't make it so big that it takes up a whole screen. That means two things: a long download time (which is boring) and the logo is taking up valuable real estate on the page that can be used for information. If you design on a computer with a 17- or 19-inch monitor, remember that most people still are looking at 12- or 15-inch screen, therefore leave blank space so people can read your page easily.

Organize your information so it is easy to retrieve. That oftentimes means tables and frames. My first rule of thumb is to look at what works on someone else's site and modify it. If I find a Web site that has a table that I like, I go to Source Code on my browser and find the code for the table. Then I block, copy, and paste it to a word processor page and put my specifics in place of theirs. After I've done that for a couple of Web pages, I begin to see the logic of the tags, and I can figure it out there. If I'm still lost, I go to the HTML Web sites I've listed above. And if that does not work, I ask my students, who can usually show me how something works. The kids have the time to play with different Web sites and tags, and they "get it" better than us oldsters can.

If you are interested in working with tables and frames, here are a few sites that will be of use. Go to the Web Designer at **http://web.canlink.com/webdesign/** and scroll to "tables" to see their user-friendly comments about design, tables, frames, animated graphics, and the like. It's a good place to look if you want to become a fairly proficient coder. Also, check out HTML Tables (part of the Home: HTML Style Guide) at **http://www.mvd.com/webguide/style2.shtml** for some great information.

I like tables and frames. They help organize information in a linear fashion. If you don't think in a linear fashion, stay away from them. They can be very complicated to code, which is why I suggest "borrowing" from another site. Frames however, are another story. A word of warning about frames: If you do not have a fast computer, or a fast connection to the web, frames will slow down a Web site. Also, if a person is using an old browser (anything before version 3.x of Microsoft Internet Explorer or Netscape) the frame might be "read" by the browser, but the page will not be readable.

While we are on the subject of making your Web site more attractive, don't forget color. You can add backgrounds that are solid colors, or with texture. You can change the color of your leading links and your followed links, as well as the color of the font (but realize that some browsers will then make the text nearly illegible). To see how to add more color to your Web site, check out the background and graphics links that 1, 2, 3 . . . Easy! has at **http://spring-board.com/123easy/map.html**.

While thinking about backgrounds, don't forget you can use graphic files. Caboodles at **http://www.caboodles.com/** has many different graphics and clip art collections from which to choose. You can search in Yahoo for any of these items. I just searched in Yahoo for "html backgrounds" and received a list of over twenty site matches.

✎ In Your Classroom

How to Build a Web Site for Your Class

Building a Web page is an excellent learning activity for your students. It encourages reading, writing, aesthetic judgment, cooperation, collaboration, creativity, and, last but not least, proofreading skills. I hope you have the opportunity to use the following lesson plan in your classroom, as it is one that has worked in many classrooms.

Goal

To design, code, and upload a home page for your class.

Rationale

You want the world to know what you are doing, and while the Web may be your window on the world, a home page is the world's window on you: Your class looks out, and the world looks in. You also want to reinforce skills in reading, writing, drawing, proof-reading, and collaborating, and instruct in the relatively new skill of coding.

Objectives

- Students will compose a meaningful message for their home page and Web site.

- Students will develop expertise in collecting, organizing, and writing data (both textual and graphical); in using HTML; and in producing and maintaining a Web site with selected links.

- Students will work collaboratively on the program.

Procedures

Designing your own home page is an excellent project for your class (or school) after everyone interested has experienced being online. When your students know a little about mining the Web for information and the types of information that are out there, they will probably have ideas for their own home page(s). Set the stage by telling your class that they can develop a short home page and put in on the local server, but that to do this, the server requires that they have a clear message and a reasonable reason for using the space—the more focused, the better; the more imaginative, the better.

At this point, brainstorm with your students to come up with the best reason for having a home page and a message for your class. One fourth-grade class has an interactive creative-writing project through which they are communicating with people all over the world. Another class is doing a global weather survey. Yet another is communicating the results of a scientific experiment that is being done in several classrooms across the United States, the United Kingdom, and New Zealand. Others just have projects that have been done by the kids. Only the scope of your imagination and your students' imaginations constrain the boundaries of your possibilities.

Spark your students' interest by finding several good examples of home pages written by classes that are similar to yours, in terms of grade level or subject, and see what your electronic neighbors have been doing. Talk over what makes an excellent home page, a so-so home page, and a not-so-good home page. Look for home pages that convey a message that is appealing yet meaningful.

Brainstorm with your class about what they would like to see on their own home page. Revisit the issue of the reason for your class having a home page, and what the message ought to be. Generate a list of ideas for possible contents. Here's a starter list:

- student stories
- interactive stories (stories that are being written online in partnership with other kids in other places)
- your class or school newspaper (this idea is further developed in Chapter 9: *The CyberNews*)
- pictures drawn by students
- collaborative projects with other classes at your school or with other schools (an invitation to become keypals or online penpals)
- a history of your school

- biographical sketches of famous people from your hometown or state

- favorite areas of study and hobbies with individual comments and questions

- science projects

- information and news about where you live, and maybe a virtual tour of the notable and scenic spots in your locality (like the one suggested in Chapter 11: *Virtually Together in D.C.*)

- pictures of everything you talk about

- audio clips and video footage (if you have the technical capacity)

- and oh! so much more

One caveat: if you provide any e-mail addresses on your Web page, realize that you are creating an open invitation to receive e-mail messages from all over the world. Be careful what information you and your students divulge to the world. They should not be telling the world their home addresses, phone numbers, and e-mail addresses without receiving prior permission.

If you are ambitious, lead your class to become the force that organizes a home page for your entire school. (In that case, your class home page will be a link on the school Web site.) To involve other classes and even the whole school means that your class will have to accept the responsibility of teaching other people about the Internet. Think about the implications of this undertaking and talk it over thoroughly with all the major players. This can be a big project.

After the brainstorming period, it's time to prioritize and develop an outline of your proposed home page before you start writing—and long before you start coding it. Without this outline, you may lose direction and focus, and end up with a hodgepodge page that visitors will visit once but never again. Remind everyone that the page is going to be on the World Wide Web. This means it will be viewed and read by possibly thousands of people all over the world, who will build their only impression of you and your interests by reading your class home page. Posting a home page via the Web to the world is awesome, your kids will agree, and a responsibility not to be taken lightly.

Display the outline on a bulletin board in your room. On this display, establish a schedule of deadlines: dates by which text has to be completed, when links have to be identified and coded, when the home page will have its test run, when it will be reviewed and modified, and a schedule when links should be updated or maintained.

Assign different parts of the project to different groups of students according to their stated interests. Allow everyone to work with as many different parts of the project—organization, text, coding, graphics, proofing, etc.—as they like, so that they can exercise their talents and skills, and take ownership of the finished product. Here's a checklist of some of the groups that are useful:

- project coordinator or Webmaster (to help you keep up with everybody else)

- information and image gatherers

- copywriters

- coders

- editors

- proofreaders

- page designers and layout artists

- artists and graphics designers

- reporters (to get stories from other classes, the principal, parents, etc.)

- maintenance staff

You will certainly need a group to communicate with the people in charge of your intended Web server (where the site will be), whether they are your school's own systems technicians, an Internet Service Provider (ISP), a nearby university, a regional freenet, or some other on-ramp to the Information Superhighway. The job of this group is to establish your right to, and the process for, uploading your home page onto their Internet server.

The group that maintains the computer files during the building process exercises critical hands-on responsibility. Not only must they manage the files of the various elements of your Web site, but they also need to keep a detailed list of all the files, with complete reference to titles, and what each title means. This is work for your detail-minded students. For example, on the first Web site I created, there were 205 separate files, each one with a different name. To remember what the file names represented, I made a master list of the file names and what was in each file. Sure I could have viewed the file to determine what was in it, but a hard copy list was easier for me to refer to. Because I shared Webmaster duties with another faculty member, we would be working at cross-purposes if we did not have our master list of files. In addition, Web pages have to be maintained and updated, and it is difficult to remember what 205 obscure titles mean, six months after they were written, especially if they were created by a number of students.

Even if your students are mature and responsible, I suggest that you will need eight arms and about the same number of eyes to keep up with all the groups and keep them focused on their tasks. Needless to say, no matter how young or old your students are, how responsible and mature, you are the Ultimate Webmaster: The buck stops with you.

After the home page is up and running, it will need a hands-on Webmaster, an individual who is responsible in every way for every aspect of an active Web site. That person will assuredly and ultimately, I repeat, be you, but it would be good developmental instruction for the students to choose the right person from their midst to be the student Webmaster of public record, your associate in this responsibility. Your student Webmaster can have as many assistant Webmasters as seems desirable. I suggest rotating the job of Webmaster among the kids competent to do the work; that way, more people can learn from the experience. Your students need to know that the class home page is not a passing fad but a high-stakes project that they are going to stick with through the entire year. I suggest, if possible, that you put a counter on your home page that keeps a record of "hits"—it tabulates how many times your home page has been visited. Seeing those hits accumulate will help to maintain interest on the part of your students. If you get hits enough to prove to a client that your Web site gets a lot of traffic, you might even sell advertising space on your home page.

Technical Production of Your Home Page

After the home page copy has been composed, and the pictures and other information are gathered and organized, the home page needs to be formatted to be readable by a browser. You will need to teach your students how to put pictures in a correct format for downloading, how to write text files using the word processor, and how to code in HTML. None of this is as difficult as it may sound; the processes are fairly simple ones. The kids who do this work, however, need to be the ones who take instruction well, who have an eye for detail, and who can follow directions.

If you are using a word processing program such as Word or WordPerfect, click on "Save As" every time you want to save a document for uploading to your Web page. Because the "Save As" function lets you save files in a variety of formats, choose "text," "text only" or "ASCII text" and then click on OK; your document is thereby saved as a plain text file. Should you happen to forget, and not save a document as a text file, it cannot be read by a browser. In addition, your browser will not be able to read any text file unless its name ends with the suffix **.html** (for Macintosh users) or **.htm** (for PC users). Therefore, a typical text file name might be "egc.html" and a typical image file name might be "egc.gif". The suffix **.html** has the function of telling the browser that the file is written in mark-up language while the suffix **.gif** tells the browser that the file contains an image. The newest versions of some word processing programs now allow you to "Save As" an HTML file. This is a real time saver.

After a document has been word-processed and saved as a text file, put your proofreaders to work. Have them check for errors in content, as well as spelling and grammar. You may want to have two groups of proofreaders, one for content and organization, another for spelling and grammar. When they have finished proofing a file, make sure that it is saved as a text file once again. You can change text in a document after it has been marked up with HTML, but it is much easier to make changes while the document is still a word processing file—before it has been coded.

Your artists and coders need to work closely together. The artists help to design the page, while the coding crew puts in the tags to the text files. You will need to show your artists how to make image files using **.gif** or **.jpg** format. This will require a scanner and a graphics program like Adobe Photoshop, which can create **.gif** or **.jpg** files from scanned art, photos, or image files.

Your coders will need to learn how to code in HyperText Mark-up Language. Earlier in the chapter you saw several HTML primers, and most of them are easy to understand. I've found quite a few other good HTML guides on the Net, so I listed a few more below:

HTML Guide	URL
Beginner's Guide to HTML	**http://www.ncsa.uiuc.edu/General/Internet/WWW/ HTMLPrimer.html**
Crash Course on HTML	**http://www.pcweek.com/eamonn/crash_course.html**
Sizzling HTML Jalfrezi	**http://www.vzone.virgin.net/sizzling.jalfrezi/iniframe.htm**
HTML version 4.0	**http://www.w3.org/pub/WWW/MarkUp/MarkUp.html**

Choose the guide that is best for your coders and for yourself. If you have a good group of direction-followers who can read documents, make sense of them, and put the directions to use, they should be able to work with any of the above HTML guides. Before you do this project, you, the teacher, need to learn it so that you can communicate with your HTML class experts. You cannot leave this task to your coders alone—they will need your assistance, especially the first time they start to code.

When you are finished putting in all the tags, it's time to put the page through a trial run in your browser program. In Netscape you do this by going to the File pull-down menu and scrolling to Open New File. Click on it and a window will appear asking where the new file is located. You locate the proper HTML file, click on it, and hit OK. Soon the Netscape screen will show the document. If it has been coded correctly, it should look just as you want it to look. If it does not look that way, then you identify the errors and go back to the drawing board. Sometimes you will have to make many, small changes in order for a file to look as you think it should look. If there are problems you can't find, you may want to use a Web-based HTML validation sites: Weblint (**http:// www.weblint.com**), Bobby (**http://www.cast.org/bobby**), or the W3C HTML Validation Service (**http://validator.w3.org/**) are three such helpers. (I've made about two perfect files in all the time I've been doing HTML—it's harder to get them perfect the first time around than you think.)

Home pages require a lot of feeding, watering, and tending; therefore, your maintenance group, including your Webmaster(s), will become more important over the long term. There are times when you will not be able to do the needed maintenance on your Web page. When, however, the information on a Web page becomes dated and incorrect, you are definitely no longer putting your best foot forward! Look at the bottom of many Web sites and you will probably see a date. This date tells you the last time the page was updated. This is important if you are trying to get the most recent information. If you have date-sensitive information or links on your home page, you will feel the need for timely maintenance even more—possibly on a weekly or even daily basis. (I'm not exaggerating! Some Web sites are updated every day. My Web page gets updated once a semester.) If, for example, your Web page talks about a big event that's going to happen in the Spring, and it's already late Summer and heading into Fall, it's past time for some home page maintenance.

Evaluation

A finished home page with an address on the Web is but one piece of evidence that the project was successful: the public component. Less obvious, but more important, are the skills that have been communicated and practiced: group participation, cooperation, and collaboration; reading, writing, drawing, layout design, proofreading, spelling and coding skills; the ability to follow directions; the honing of attention to detail; and the individual personal responsibility required to achieve presentable work for public display. Your class will have met a full spectrum of opportunities to learn in every aspect of the curriculum. Putting a home page up on the Web gives new meaning to the phrase "across the curriculum."

Included at the end of this chapter is a rubric for evaluating a student-made Web page. It was modified from the one found at "Tammy's Tech Tips for Teachers" at **http:// www.sv400.k12.ks.us/tips/Web pagerubric.html**.

Things You Don't Want to Do

I would be remiss if I did not mention some of my pet peeves about Web page construction. I'm sure you have seen Web pages that are just too busy, have a terrible background color, or have just too much stuff on them. Think about those things that really bother you when you visit a Web site, and try not to make those mistakes. Here are some design problems that really bother me:

1. **Scrolling Texts, Marquees, and Constantly Running Animations.** I find these pages very distracting. A Web site with moving images on it makes me want to click to another site fast. I use the Web to find information, not to see Times Square.

2. **Complex URLs.** You know what I mean—the URLs that seem to go on forever and ever. As you know, URLs have to be typed perfectly, so the chance of making a typo is greater with a long or complex list of meaningless letters, than with a short list of sensible abbreviations. Try to use short names with all lowercase characters and no special characters such as # or $.

3. **Long Download Times.** Sites that have lots of graphics or exceptionally large audio/video files take too long to download, especially for a school setting. If it takes too long to get the information, students become bored. You don't need that!

4. **Dead Pages and Outdated Information.** A dead page is one that has just disappeared from the Web without a forwarding address. There are also Web pages that have not changed for several years. Avoid catching this malady.

5. **Long Index or Home Pages.** Somewhere I read that only ten percent of all users scroll beyond the information that is visible on the screen when the page comes up. That's why I like critical content and navigation options on the top part of the home page.

6. **Blinking Pages.** Last but not least, I cannot stand pages that blink at me. At first I thought they were fun, and I made a few, but as I see more of them out there on the Web, I'm sorry I ever liked them at all. I find them very

annoying, especially if I'm trying to read something near the blinking. Blinks would be okay if the user could turn them off! I also do not like distracting animations on a page (and I really dislike flashing advertisements, but they usually do not appear on school pages).

To test your mastery of HTML, you can take the tutorial developed by Eric Meyer at Case Western Reserve University. Turn on your browser and open **http://www.cwru.edu/help/introHTML/**. (By the way, Eric has been a guest "speaker" on my Indiana class several times. Eric knows HTML and makes it easy to understand. He also proofread this chapter. Thank you, Eric!)

I hope you enjoyed learning HTML. Whether or not you get your class Web page up and running, send me some e-mail about what you are doing with the Internet. You can reach me via e-mail at **cotton@instruction.com**. Tell me about your class, and what they have been doing with the Internet. I'll write back!

See you on the Web!

Evaluation Rubric for Creating a Web Page

Assessment Area	Exceptional	Good	Fair	Needs Improvement
Layout / Design	• Well organized • Eye catching • Uses special features like tables • Text spacing and alignment make reading easy • Backgrounds enhance the page	• Attractive page • Good organization of text and graphics • Easy to read text • Backgrounds are appropriate	• Page appears "busy" or "boring" • Text may be difficult to read • Backgrounds somewhat distracting	• Unattractive pages • Text difficult to read • Distracting backgrounds
Art/Graphics	• Photos, icons, and clip art are used creatively and follow a theme	• Photos, icons, and clip art are appropriate, of high quality, and download fairly quickly	• Photos are blurry or fuzzy • Icons and clip art do not "fit" topic. • Too many pictures make download time slow	• No photos, icons or clip art • Inappropriate or of low quality photos, icons or clip art
Information	• Creatively written and cleverly presented	• Well written information • Interesting to read and use • Information is not too long or too short per section	• Information is not written well • Too much information is given per section	• Poorly written, inaccurate, or incomplete information
Navigation/Links	• Links are created with images and icons to enhance the text links • All links consistently work	• All links work and easy to find • Page is not confusing as the user can navigate back and forth through pages	• Some links are dead • Page is confusing to user	• Links are dead or inaccurate • The user may become confused or bored
Working Together	• Teammates show respect for one another • Get along well • Work together on all aspects of the project	• Teammates get along well • Teammates share equally in all responsibilities	• Teammates have trouble solving disagreements • One team member does most of work	• Teammates argue much of the time • Responsibilities are not shared
Following Classroom Guidelines	• Teammates are always on task, stay in their own area, and cause no disruptions	• Teammates stay in their area, talk quietly to their teammates only • Teammates cause minimum disruptions	• Teammates occasionally leave area without permission • Teammates are louder than necessary	• Teammates are often out of area without permission • Teammates cause disruptions

Modified from Tammy's Tech Tips for Teachers at http://www.essdack.org/tips/webpagerubric.html.

Chapter 5
Using the Internet for Teaching— Rules for the Road

I bet you can hardly wait to get started! You know how to use a Web browser, and you've just visited over one hundred fantastic Web sites for teachers. You've learned how to search the Web and you've seen what it takes to code a Web page. It's just about time to get your students involved in a lesson or two. And it's just about that easy! There are some other concerns to think about, though, and they are the focus of this chapter: 1) child safety on the Internet; 2) Acceptable Use Policies (AUPs); 3) classroom management; and 4) lesson planning. While these are not nearly as much fun as looking at Web sites and deciding what you are going to do with them, they are important if you want to use the Internet as an effective tool for instruction. By the way, the Internet is just one more tool for instruction. It is not the curriculum.

A Discussion on Child Safety on the Internet

Are your students going to be safe when they walk the Web? Should you censor the material on the Internet that comes into your classroom, or should you let your students use their conscience as their guide? That's a question you have to answer for your own group of students. I am not in favor of censorship, but my situation is different from yours, so I cannot make your decision. I can, however, offer the following "work arounds" that might be helpful.

The Internet is a human invention. It was developed by adults, for military, academic, and scientific purposes. It was never designed to be a children's playground. The Internet is the largest international storehouse of information, accessed by hundreds of thousands of people every hour of the day and night. There are no Internet police. There is no one person or group telling you what you can and cannot do. As an international entity, it is hard to police. There are some acts that, if caught, are illegal (at least in the U.S.). Because of this, some Web sites on the Internet are not appropriate for children, or even for all adults. You can be sure that your students will find—maybe even search for—the good, the bad and the ugly on the Internet. Cyberporn, advocacy of violence, invitations to buy things that are prohibited to underage people, inappropriate e-mail invitations from people with perverted intentions for the naive and innocent—all of this, and other bad stuff, is mixed in together with the good stuff I showed you earlier on the Internet. Depending on what you read these days, there are "tons of smut" on the Internet, and there is no way to protect yourself or your kids—whether your own children or your students—from it. What do I think? There are millions of Web pages on the Internet, and I believe that the good outweighs the evil. However, if you want, you can purchase or download blocking and filtering programs that censor unwanted materials.

In classrooms where teachers use the Internet all the time, they tell their students not to view objectionable sites, and they regularly monitor their students' use of the computers. To this end, many teachers have a set of "ground rules" that are posted regarding objectionable Web sites. These ground rules are similar to Acceptable Use Policies, which I'll talk about in the next section. Just like we don't close libraries because there are some banned books, we do not want to stop all access to the Internet just because of some questionable sites. It is part of our job as educators to teach young people how to cope with the unhappy realities of life. I believe that teachers and parents need to tell their kids what they ought and ought not to do, and then make the consequences of violating the rules fit the behavior. That's discipline. That's education.

As a teacher, you can do a lot to help kids cope with the bad stuff in their world, including the bad stuff that assails them on the Net. You need to encourage your students to stay on the right track, as well as to be forthright with them in discussing the dangers that lurk, have always lurked, and shall forever lurk, out there in reality. I've asked many teachers and parents what they say to their kids. The following speech is more or less the essence of what many teachers say:

> *"There's good stuff and bad stuff on the Internet. I give you free access to the good stuff, but I ask you to respect your fellow classmates—and me—and stay away from the questionable side of the Net. Please do not let me catch you surfing at restricted sites, as I will be forced to take action that will be harmful to you. If you do not understand why pornography, violence, and other abuses are bad for you, stop by my desk after class and let's talk it over."*

If that speech is not going to work for your students, then please consider some of the blocking and filtering programs that are available. There are at least three varieties of programs that allow you to control what your students can view on the Web. You can block Web sites, filter Web sites and monitor Web sites.

Blocking programs allow you to stop access to IRC-Chat lines, News Groups, File Transfer Protocol (FTP), and e-mail attachments. Filtering programs allow you to separate out files that are offensive, such as sexually oriented or adult Web sites, Web sites advocated illegal activities, Web sites that are violent, or Web sites that advocate hate or intolerance. Monitoring programs keep track of where your students have been on the Web, how long, and, in some cases, provide a printout telling you of the exact Web sites visited.

There are many of these programs available. Many of them are multi-functional, doing blocking, filtering and monitoring; some only have one or two functions. Listed below are the URLs for the most commonly used programs.

SurfWatch at **http://www1.surfwatch.com** is a filtering program. It has a database of 100,000 Web sites that it rates using five core categories—Drugs/Alcohol/Tobacco, Gambling, Hate Speech, Sexually Explicit, and Violence—as well as ChatBlock. You can download a fifteen-day free trial version of the program, and once you buy the program, you can download free upgrades.

Cyber Patrol at **http://www.cyberpatrol.com/** is a filtering program too. It has the CyberNOT and CyberYES list of Web sites. The folks at Cyber Patrol screen Web sites according to Violence/Profanity; Partial Nudity; Full Nudity; Sexual Acts; Gross Depictions; Intolerance; Satanic/Cult; Drug/Drug Culture; Militant/Extremist; Sex Education; Questionable/Illegal and Gambling; and Alcohol and Tobacco. You can download a free trial version of Cyber Patrol for both Macintosh and PC platforms.

Net Nanny at **http://www.netnanny.com/netnanny/** is a filtering program. I could not find a list of what it filters. You can download a free thirty-day trial version without Net Nanny technical support.

CyberSnoop at **http://www.pearlsw.com/csnoop/edu/ descript.htm** is a monitoring program. It was designed with the "philosophy that while we trust our children, we must have a means to supervise and guide them." Like the other programs, you can download a free trial version for Windows 95 or NT.

CyberSitter at **http://www.solidoak.com/index.html** is a blocking, filtering and monitoring program. You can download a ten-day trial version of the program. You can block certain types of Web sites (IRC, ftp://, e-mail attachments, etc.) and you can filter Web sites according to violence, language, sex and illegal activities.

Lastly, if you are using MSIE (Microsoft Internet Explorer) as your browser, take advantage of the built-in filtering program. To find it, go to your pull-down menus and click on Tools and scroll to Internet Options. Click on the Content Tab and scroll to Content Advisor and click on Enable settings. After typing in a password, you can filter Web sites according to RASCI (Recreational Software Advisory Council of the Internet) guidelines for Violence, Nudity, Sex, and Language. To find out more about these guidelines, go to **http://www.rsac.org/ratingsv01.html**.

All blocking, filtering and monitoring programs are password protected, meaning you can turn off and on the password, as you wish. Therefore, if you want to walk the Web without the benefit of the program, you can turn it off.

You might want to think about having a parent's night at your school where the teachers can explain what is being done to protect their children from freely going to X-rated places on the Internet. As with so many other topics available on the Internet, there are Web sites devoted to child safety. One of the best Web sites is at Yahooligans, at **http://www.yahooligans.com/docs/safety**, called "Staying Street Smart on the Web." Please read what it has to say about keeping your students safe when they are online.

The Direct Marketing Association has some excellent Web pages on child safety and the Internet. Go to **http://www.the-dma.org/topframe/index7.html**. At this framed site you will find information about the many blocking programs available. They also have a twenty-four-page booklet called "Cybersavvy" (**http://www.cybersavvy.org/**) that is worth reading.

You may also want to think about subscribing to an online, server-based filter that ensures child safety. Bess: The Internet Retriever for Kids, Families and Schools at **http://www.n2h2.com/bess-noframes.htm** is one such provider. If you live in Western Washington state, you can be an individual subscriber to Bess. If you are a school district (anywhere) interested in this service, dial into Bess, just as you dial into your online server now, and instead of using Netscape, you use the Bess Browser. Bess offers links to preselected Web sites, plus you can block entire Web sites or individual pages within a Web site. In addition, incoming and outgoing e-mail is screened for inappropriate language. Lastly, the service is continually updated with the promise to add more than 20,000 acceptable Web sites a month. There is a monthly fee for subscribing to Bess, but a service such as this can provide peace of mind. Some teachers like it, while some teachers complain that it automatically puts up a wall of distrust. These are issues that you have to decide for your own class and school.

One last word about Internet safety. You want your students to be familiar with working on the Internet, yet you do not have enough computers networked or online. There is an answer to this dilemma: Use an offline browser program.

Offline browsers allow you to copy complete Web sites from the Web and use them with your students without being online at the time. WebBuddy (**http://www.dataviz.com/Products/WebBuddy/ WB_Home.html**), and WebWhacker from Blue Squirrel at **http:// www.bluesquirrel.com/products/whacker/whacker.html** are two such programs. A program similar to WebWhacker is the Offline Educator (also made by Blue Squirrel). It does the same thing, only for an entire classroom of networked computers. See Offline Educator at **http://www.bluesquirrel.com/products/educator/ educator.html**.

With any of these programs, you can select a Web site that enhances your lesson, or copy the whole Web site, including all or some of the connecting links, graphics, video, audio, etc. To use the copy, all you need is a computer with the correct browser program (these programs work with either Netscape Navigator or Internet Explorer), and of course the offline browser program. You do not need to be online to view the stored site. For schools with a limited number of computers and online time, this is a perfect solution. It is also a good way to use a lesson time and again, and be sure that the Web site does not change focus or URL. I have a collection of great Web sites that I have "WebWhacked," or copied, that I use when I demonstrate lessons to groups of students. With an offline browser program, I don't have to worry if I can get online, if a Web site is busy, or if there is questionable material on the Web site. I have control of all of those issues.

Starting with Version 5.0 of MSIE, there is an offline browser capability. When you see a Web site that you want to copy, click on Favorites, then tell MSIE that you want to be able to view the Web site while you are offline. Like the other programs mentioned above, it will take a bit of time to collect all the graphics and text and connected URLs, but the end product is a Web site you can view without being online.

Acceptable Use Policies

While blocking, filtering and monitoring programs are available—as are safety tips and offline browsers—it is still mandatory to have an Acceptable Use Policy. Given the above, what are some actions that you can do to make the Internet accessible, while keeping your students safe when they are online. As stated above, there are sites out in cyberspace that are X-rated—or worse. While these make up about five percent of the Web sites found on the Net, your students will find them quickly. You need to discuss censorship, and you and your school need to have in place an Acceptable Use Policy and/or Student Safety Policy to help assure parents, community members, and the students that you want your students to be safe on the Information Superhighway.

Acceptable Use Policies (AUPs) tell all the stakeholders that you are using the Internet for educational and curricular purposes. You need an Acceptable Use Policy for the following reasons:

- AUPs educate your students and their parents about the tools and programs that will be used on the Internet, and what can be expected from those tools and programs in a very general way.

- AUPs define boundaries for Internet behavior and misbehavior.

- AUPs specify consequences that the system administrator might take in order to maintain the network. This way, there are no surprises during the school year.

There are many sample AUPs on the Web. Take a look at a number of them written by other teachers in other school districts before writing one and having it approved by your school. See some of these sites for Acceptable Use Policies:

- Armadillo Acceptable Use Policies at **http:// chico.rice.edu/armadillo/acceptable.html**

- Nancy Willard's K–12 Acceptable Use Policy Template at **http://www.erehwon.com/k12aup/**

From the above lists you will see many examples, but I particularly like the AUP developed by the Los Angeles Unified School

District in California at **http://www.lausd.k12.ca.us/ welcome.html**, which is included at the end of this chapter. You have permission to make copies of this AUP, so copy it and read what it has to say. Based on my experience from my Internet class at Indiana University and schools around the country, AUPs that are not filled with legalese seem to be easier to understand and enforce. This is one of many things to keep in mind.

Most AUPs have the following points in common: 1.) Standards for security and safety; 2.) Guidelines about the amount of time allowed on the Internet, who is responsible for enforcing the AUP, and Netiquette (network etiquette); 3.) Consequences for misbehavior; and 4.) Consent forms to be signed by parents/guardians and the student. Recently I've seen some schools add a "non-consent" line to the form, which gives parents the option to not give their children the privilege of using the Internet for instructional purposes. The option of not giving consent is important too. Usually, when an Acceptable Use Policy has been signed by the parents or guardians, either with consent or non-consent, the form is kept as part of a permanent record with the rest of the child's files.

After your school committee has developed the AUP, and it is approved by the board and your lawyers, inform your students, their parents and everyone else about your policies. Have your students and their parents sign the AUP, and then stick to it. I know this is difficult to do, especially if one of your kids breaks the policy, but it has to be done. There is a lot of concern about kids getting into X-rated or questionable Web sites, and you need to have an AUP in place to assure parents that you are not aiding and abetting any questionable situations. I am not for censorship on the Internet, as I am not for censorship of books, because, like a library, the Internet has a wealth of information meant for all people. I am for teaching kids the appropriate Internet behavior they have to use in the classroom. An AUP can help enforce and regulate the expected behavior.

To enhance your AUP, think about adding one further requirement: Taking and passing of an Internet Test and earning an Internet Driver's License (IDL). This might sound like a gimmick, but it does inform your students you are serious about enforcing the rules and regulations for accessing the Internet in your classroom. One of the teachers I work with has developed a Safety Surf Test, which you can see at **http:// meltingpot.fortunecity.com/myanmar/255/index.html**.

I generally have students and parents read and sign the Acceptable Use Policy. Then I have the students take a test on the AUP. When they pass the test, they receive an Internet Driver's License, which is good for a specified period of time (usually one school year). In order to log on to a computer at school, the kids must display their IDL. It's a promise from my students that they are going to follow the AUP to the best of their abilities. A sample of a generic Internet test and IDL that you may copy are at the end of this chapter.

Ten Classroom Management Guidelines

When your students and their parents have signed the consent form on the AUP and your students have passed the AUP Test, you need to give your students time to practice using the computer and the Internet. They need it as much as you did when you were first accessing the Web. This is where you have to think about managing the Internet classroom.

Listed below are a set of guidelines that I've collected from many of the 150 classrooms I've visited in the past couple of years. Some of them might be helpful to you.

1. Set aside some Internet time (or reserve the computer lab) on a regular basis, so your students will have time to practice and learn. If you have a one-modem classroom, you may use the sample schedule on page 115.

2. Face computer monitors so you can see the screens. When you can see what the students are doing, they are more likely to stay on task.

3. Enlarge the font size on your browser. If you use Netscape, go to Options in the pull-down menus, then General Preferences, and finally Fonts. Change the size from 12 to 24. With MSIE, click on the font button until you see the largest font size available. As with #2 above, if you can see what your students are doing, they are more likely to do what they are supposed to do.

4. Assign students to work in groups of two or three. Small groups allow for collaboration and teamwork to occur. It makes for better use of your limited Internet resource and the old saying "two heads are better than one," really works when you are teaching with the Internet.

5. Assign each computer in your room a name (or number). I've seen computers named "Skywalker" and "Baby," as well as "Joanie" and "Scott." The kids seem to like the names, as it gives them ownership, and it makes identifying the computers so much easier, especially if there is a problem. ("Mrs. Cotton, Skywalker can't get online today, what's the matter with it?" is sometimes heard.)

6. If you have classroom computers, create an online schedule or calendar. A sample schedule for intermediate grades is on the following pages.

7. Consider using headphones or turning the sound to low or off, depending on your room size, the location of your computers, and your level of noise tolerance.

8. Make sure all of your computers have the same browser. (I know this sounds logical, but I've been in rooms that have three different browsers and that just makes your job so much harder to do.)

9. Reset the home page to one of two topics: your favorite search engine or directory (many intermediate teachers have the home page set for Yahooligans at **http:// www.yahooligans.com**/, while middle school and high school teachers have it set for AltaVista at **http:// altavista.digital.com**); or to the URL you want all of your students to visit so they can start a particular lesson.

10. Ask your students to use "inch voices" when they are working online. A "three-inch voice" is one that can be heard three inches away; a "twelve-inch voice" can be heard twelve inches away. You get the idea. Whatever the case, expect *some* noise. Interaction is important.

Sample Two-Week Schedule for One-Modem Self-Contained Classrooms

	MON	WED	FRI	MON	WED	FRI
9:00 – 9:45	Group 1	Group 5	Group 1	Group 5	Group 1	Group 5
10:00 – 10:45	Group 2	Group 6	Group 2	Group 6	Group 2	Group 6
11:00 – 11:45	Group 3	Group 7	Group 3	Group 7	Group 3	Group 7
1:00 – 1:45	Group 4	Group 8	Group 4	Group 8	Group 4	Group 8

This schedule allows for a group of students (usually no more than 4) to work on one online computer for about 45 minutes, 2 days a week. When this schedule is published ahead of time, there seems to be little or no confusion.

Sample Schedule for Self-Contained Classrooms with 4 Online Connections

	COMPUTER 1	COMPUTER 2	COMPUTER 3	COMPUTER 4
9:00 – 9:45	Group 1	Group 2	Group 3	Group 4
10:00 – 10:45	Group 5	Group 6	Group 7	Group 8
11:00 – 11:45	Group 9	Group 10	Group 11	Group 12

If you have four computers that can be online at the same time, it pays to have smaller groups of students and more groups. This schedule is set up for 45-minute work sessions. The student groups are small, this time, only two or three per group. With four computers online at the same time, there will need to be a set of "ground rules" decided upon by the teacher and / or students as to behavior, etiquette, etc. The students can work as many days online as possible. If the computers are in your classroom, I recommend going online at least three times a week. This gives the students needed practice.

When I'm first working with students on the Internet, I assign groups. As I get to know what each student can do, I then let the students self-assign. Self-assignment into groups is a privilege, not a right, and I let my students know that.

One Final Word about Safety

If you are using the Web and get repeated unsolicited e-mails, you can stop it. Go to the FBI Web site at **http://www.fbi.gov/fo/fo.htm** and tell them about it. If you want quicker action, call them at 1-800-843-5678. Check out their Internet Safety Tips at **http://www.fbi.gov/kids/internet/internet.htm**, and their Parent's Guide to Internet Safety at **http://www.fbi.gov/tips.htm**. Both are excellent, and both are available as a brochure which you can give to your parents.

Summary

None of the above is easy or fun. But they are all necessary. When you are using the Internet in your classroom, *you* are the bottom line. You want your students to learn in a safe environment. In most schools you can control that environment in many subtle ways. It is difficult to control the Internet, as it is not self-contained like your school site is. It is a network of thousands of servers, with millions of Web sites generated by children and adults from every corner of our world. Given that, it is not humanly possibly to control what your students have access to without some help. An Acceptable Use Policy will give you and your students guidance. Blocking, filtering and monitoring programs can provide some peace of mind. And solid instructional strategies in lesson planning and management will bring you one step closer to using the Internet as another instructional tool.

Copied with Permission from the Los Angeles Unified School District Information Technology Division
http://www.lausd.k12.ca.us/welcome.html (then click on "AUP")

Acceptable Use Policy (AUP) for LAUSDnet

I. BACKGROUND

The Internet, a network of networks, allows people to interact with hundreds of thousands of networks and computers. All connections to the Internet by Los Angeles Unified School District (LAUSD) students or employees are subject to the LAUSD's Acceptable Use Policy (AUP).

Access to the Internet allows connections to computer systems located all over the world. Users (and parents of student users) must understand that neither the District nor any LAUSD employee controls the content of the information found on these systems. Some of the information may be controversial and may even be offensive to some individuals. Teachers or other school personnel should ensure that connections to the Internet are used in a responsible, efficient, ethical, and legal manner, and such use must be in support of education and research consistent with LAUSD's educational objectives.

II. INTERNET ACCESS

The Internet is a public network, and as such, e-mail is not private. LAUSDnet system operators have access to all user account directories and data, e-mail, personal web pages, and any other files stored on system servers. System operators may delete files at any time to conform to system storage needs.

LAUSDnet Internet services must be a free and open forum for expression. Any statement of personal belief in e-mail or other posted material is understood to be the author's individual point of view, and not that of the Los Angeles Unified School District, the administrators of LAUSDnet, or any LAUSD office or school. However, since LAUSDnet access is provided as an instructional tool rather than a personal forum, users will not use LAUSDnet access to demean, defame, or denigrate others for race, religion, creed, color, national origin, ancestry, physical handicap, gender, sexual persuasion, or other reasons.

III. LAUSDnet ACCEPTABLE USE POLICY RULES AND REGULATIONS

Access to the Internet from LAUSDnet and the receipt of an LAUSDnet account is a privilege, not a right. Access to LAUSDnet is free to actively enrolled students, with a Student Identification Number, and to active LAUSD employees. Each user, as well as a minor's parent or guardian, voluntarily agrees to release, hold harmless, defend, and indemnify, the Los Angeles Unified School District, its officers, board members, employees, and agents, for and against all claims, actions, charges, losses or damages which arise out of the user's use of LAUSDnet, including, but not limited to negligence, personal injury, wrongful death, property lose or damage, delays, non-deliveries, mis-deliveries of data, or service interruptions.

(continued on next page)

Each user acknowledges that the information available from other websites may not be accurate. Use of any of the information obtained via the Internet is at the user's own risk. Los Angeles Unified District makes no warranty of any kind, either express or implied, regarding the quality, accuracy or validity of the data on the Internet.

The LAUSDnet AUP Rules and Regulations are listed below:

- The person to whom a LAUSDnet account is issued is responsible at all times for its proper use.
- Any inappropriate use may result in the cancellation of the privilege of use, and/or disciplinary action.
- Any district employee who uses LAUSDnet inappropriately is subject to disciplinary action, including dismissal.
- LAUSDnet users should change their password frequently.
- LAUSDnet users shall not give their password information to another user nor allow another user to utilize their account.
- Students may obtain accounts on LAUSDnet only through a teacher sponsor at the school at which they are enrolled, after they have successfully completed the Student Internet test.
- The teacher sponsor must obtain and follow the required District procedures for student accounts. Please refer to the LAUSDnet Student Access packet.
- All student users, who access the Internet from any District facility or from a remote location that connects with any District facility, must have a STUDENT SIGNATURE AND PARENTAL RELEASE form on file at the school. This form is to be renewed on an annual basis.
- Home use of LAUSDnet by students, must be supervised by parents and parents are completely responsible for the student's use of the Internet resources from home.
- Schools may supplement any provisions of the District AUP, and may require additional parent releases and approvals, but in no case will such documents replace the District STUDENT SIGNATURE AND PARENTAL CONSENT RELEASE form.
- Active LAUSD employees may obtain accounts by submitting a LAUSDnet account application to Information Technology Division.

IV. ACCEPTABLE USES OF THE INTERNET INCLUDE, BUT ARE NOT LIMITED TO

- Access and use of the Internet is for use in a regular instructional activity or to compile data necessary for research needed in District schools or offices. It is the user's responsibility not to initiate access to material that is obscene, as defined in CA Penal Code section 311(a), or inconsistent with the goals, objectives, policies, and the educational mission of the District.
- A responsible user of the Internet may keep their LAUSDnet account during the time that the user is an active employee or student in LAUSD.
- A responsible user of the Internet, from any LAUSD facility, or from a remote location that connects with any LAUSD facility, may use the Internet to:
  - Conduct research
  - Communicate with other Internet users
  - Explore other computer systems
  - Post information for access by others
  - Create and maintain a personal, school, cluster or office website

(continued on next page)

V. UNACCEPTABLE USES OF THE INTERNET INCLUDE, BUT ARE NOT LIMITED TO

- Violating any state and/or federal law (i.e., copyright laws).
- Violating the California Education Code
- Using profanity, obscenity, or other language that may offensive to other users.
- Making personal attacks on other people, organizations, religions, or ethnicities.
- Harassing another person (i.e., using the Internet in a manner that bothers another person and not stopping when asked to do so by the other person).
- Sending or posting false or defamatory information about a person, group or organization which might injure the reputation of that person, group, or organization.
- Not respecting the privacy of a person by posting personal contact information, such as work or home address, telephone, e-mail address, photographs, or names, without obtaining prior permission from the person affected.
- Student information (as above) shall be posted ONLY WITH TEACHER AND PARENT PERMISSION, when this is necessary to receive information for instructional purposes.
- Forwarding personal communication without the author's prior consent.
- Using text, graphics, sound or animation in messages or the creation of WEB pages without displaying a notice, crediting the original producer of the material, and stating how permission to use the material was obtained.
- Using the resources of LAUSDnet or any other LAUSD Internet connection, including a connection from a campus network or through dial-up, to attempt unauthorized access to any other computer system, or to go beyond the user's authorized access on LAUSDnet or any other District network. This includes attempting to log in through another person's account or access another person's files. It also includes any attempts to disrupt any computer system performance or destroy data on any computer system.
- Using the Internet for commercial purposes, financial gain, personal business, produce advertisement, business service endorsement, or religious or political lobbying is prohibited.
- Using LAUSDnet, from a campus network or through dial up access, to get an e-mail account or Web page hosting privileges on another service provider.

Internet Driver's License

This license certifies that:

_____

knows the **Acceptable Use Policy** and follows
the Internet guidelines for our school.

_____

Teacher Signature

Date: _____   *Exp. Date:* _____

(This license may be reduced by 50% either before or after being completed.)

Student Internet Test

Name: _____ Date: _____

True or False (circle the correct answer)

1. It is OK to share your password with your friends. **T** or **F**

2. Copyrighted material may be downloaded from the
   Internet as long as it is cited properly. **T** or **F**

3. A student or teacher may not use the Internet to sell anything. **T** or **F**

4. It is all right to swear or verbally abuse anyone using e-mail. **T** or **F**

5. You should delete files, including old e-mail messages, from
   your account to save space on the computer. **T** or **F**

6. You should use the Internet as a tool for learning. **T** or **F**

7. Using the Internet is a privilege, not a right, and inappropriate
   use will result in cancellation of that privilege. **T** or **F**

Multiple Choice: (circle the correct answer)

8. If you think that someone is using
   your password,

   a) change your password
   b) notify the teacher or network
      administrator
   c) don't worry about it
   d) both a) and b)

9. When using e-mail, you
   a) may send letters to anyone and
      say anything
   b) may send e-mail for fun to anyone
   c) never know who is reading your mail
   d) must remember the Acceptable
      Use Policy
   e) both c) and d)

10. If you need help,
    a) ask the network operator or
       your teacher
    b) look for help on the Internet
    c) experiment
    d) all of the above
    e) none of the above

11. When you and your parents/guardians
    signed the AUP you agreed to:
    a) use the Internet for instructional
       purposes
    b) stay away from objectionable
       Web sites
    c) not download programs
    d) not waste time playing games on
       the computer
    e) all of the above

On the back of this page, in your own words write a summary of our Acceptable Use Policy.

*Modified from the Los Angeles Unified School District Acceptable Use Policy at
http://www.lausd.k12.ca.us/welcome.html (then click on "AUP").*

Chapter 6

Online in Your Classroom

Where to start? That is always a dilemma. You have just read about how to use a browser, learned how to search the Internet, and you've visited some great Web sites. You've had a taste of the language of the Web (HTML) and you've learned the basic rules for the road. That is all good background knowledge. Now you have to design curriculum in order for it to "make sense" for your classroom. Where do you start?

I like to start with teacher-based lessons and lead up to student-based lessons. Scaffold your lessons so that your students are successful. Always remember that Murphy lives on the Internet: if something can go wrong, it will. Therefore, I want my students to feel like they can succeed. If the lessons are designed from simple to difficult, each with skills that build upon what has already by used and learned, then my students will be able to do anything.

Teacher-based lessons are very directed. You are giving step-by-step instruction as to what comes first, second, and so on. This is the time when you can demonstrate the learning process and model appropriate Internet behavior. You can teach netiquette (or how to be polite on the Web). You can also reinforce the concept of sharing and collaboration. When my students are on the Web, they have to share the computer (there are not enough to go around for everyone to work individually). You can also teach the rules of the road during these demonstration lessons. Here is your opportunity to teach your students more about the Internet Driver's License and online safety.

Start out with simple lessons, where your kids have to find information from a particular page on the Web. Some of the teachers I work with like to start out using The History Channel at **http://www.history.com**, as everyday there is a different historical event mentioned. Over a period of a couple of weeks, the students can look at the page and discover something novel each time. Another good starting point is KidsClick! Have your students keep an Internet log of where they have visited. On the log, have them write the title of the Web page, the URL, and what they learned. This is just a simple recording procedure, but when they are working on bibliographies for a report it is essential. As you read the lessons that follow, you will see sample Internet logs that you can use.

After a few "find on a Web page" lessons, let your students work on scavenger hunts, where they can practice working with a directory and a keyword search engine. We've found that third graders can use Yahooligans (**http://www.yahooligans.com**) quite easily. They can also work with WebCrawler, as it is one of the easier-to-use search engines. Other search tools are mentioned in Chapter Three.

From scavenger hunts, progress to a small project or report, such as a Top Ten List, or a Hit List (explained below). This is where your students are gaining in their online knowledge, and the lessons can start to become more student-directed. Unlike the step-by-step instruction that is needed for teacher-based lessons, these lessons have a set of guidelines for the students to follow. The guidelines can be demonstrated for the kids, but thereafter they are on their own. From experience, we have found that deadlines are necessary. Depending on the class and the students, you might want to have daily or weekly deadlines. Every class is different, but because these lessons are student-based, due dates are sometimes "forgotten," and you know what that means—more work for you, the teacher.

After Top Ten Lists and Hit Lists, have students work on small reports using pen and paper, or electronic presentation programs. From there, have them work on ABC books that are more complicated. Next comes Issues reports, where they are no longer presenting facts and details, they are analyzing and synthesizing information into something that is new to them. From there go to WebQuests and Problem Based Learning, where you give your students a problem to solve.

Student-based lessons are the goal. This is indirect instruction at it's best. You give your students the goal for the lesson, the objectives or outcomes for the lesson, a choice of how to deliver the end product of the lesson, and a rubric on how the project is going to be graded. Student-based lessons stimulate divergent thinking. You will soon find out that there is not one correct answer to the lessons but, instead, many correct responses. These lessons are hard to evaluate, and that is why a rubric is necessary.

Every one of the lessons in this book follows this procedure. There is a goal, objectives/outcomes, basic procedures, and a rubric. What is not included is the type of project or product that you want your students to produce.

Stages of Development

So you start out with teacher-based lessons, with the idea of leading up to student-based lessons. You begin with simple lessons that scaffold one upon the other, leading up to more complex lessons. A bit later in this chapter there is a list of lessons for your reference. The hard part now is to find out where your students are in their own Internet growth and development. What follows is a "Stages of Development Plan" that we've been working on for awhile. (When I say we, I mean the teachers in the field, and my Indiana University and California State University Chico students—most of them practicing teachers.)

Beginning Stage	• reading and writing skills • keyboarding skills • learning a word processing program • using a word processing program • learning a browser program • learning an e-mail program (built into the browser)
Novice Stage	• multi-tasking among a word processing, browser and/or e-mail program • finding a specific Web site (when the URL is given) • using search tools such as a Web directory and a keyword search engine • using Boolean operators • using other delimiters to find information

Intermediate Step 1	• creating an individual report or project
	• collecting information
	• formatting information in a logical fashion
	• writing information for oral report, notebook, or electronic presentation using one of the following:
	  • KidPix™
	  • PowerPix™
	  • PowerPoint™
	  • HyperStudio™

Intermediate Step 2	• collaborating with others and creating a report or project
	• collecting information
	• formatting information
	• writing information for oral or multimedia delivery using one of the following:
	  • KidPix™
	  • PowerPix™
	  • PowerPoint™
	  • HyperStudio™

Advanced Stage	• creating Web pages using HTML (either using a HTML program or not) • publishing reports and projects on the Internet for others to read and make comments upon • publishing collaborative stories on the Internet for others to read and make comments upon • working on a collaborative project over time, and publishing the results on the Web
Mentoring Stage	• teaching others how to become fluent at using the Internet • troubleshooting online problems for students and teachers • troubleshooting project questions for students

To use this chart, think of what your students can do now. Pinpoint that on the chart and see what comes next on the list. This will give you an idea of where your students will go next, using the I+1 (individual plus one) principle of teaching: that of taking them from where they are, and adding just one more thing that is a bit more difficult.

Lesson Planning

You now have a basic idea of how to start lessons and to find out where your students are in their levels of Internet development. Next comes creating the lessons. This is not easy, either! Look at state frameworks or standards; look at school or district guidelines; look at your particular curriculum standards that you follow during the course of the year. From that list, select the themes and/or topics that seem to fit best with an online experience. The lessons in this book have been selected from various state frameworks in Social Studies, Science, and English/Language Arts. Each lesson is based on one particular area found in the curriculum. While it is fun to teach knowledge that is outside of the curriculum framework of the school or state, there just is not enough time in the day to do so. The best lessons are integrated with several subject areas, and are usually based on a topic or theme.

Plan your lessons with a goal, rationale, objectives/outcomes, procedures to follow, and an evaluation rubric. A goal is what you want your students to learn, know, or understand by the end of the lesson. The rationale is two-fold: why you want your students to learn this information and why they are using the Internet to learn the information! Both are needed. The objectives/outcomes are what you want your students to do to prove that they have reached the goal. The objectives/outcomes can be evaluated using a multi-step rubric that looks at mastery of the subject, mechanics, collaboration, online effectiveness, etc. Each of the lessons has a sample rubric for you to follow. The procedures are going to be different for everyone. For this book, I've written some procedures that have worked for us—but they might not work for you. Look at them, and pick and choose that which fits you the best.

Projects For Your Students

Online education relies on reading and writing. If your kids are going to gather information online, they are going to be reading. If they are going to develop a project or product, they are going to be writing. Therefore, projects need to reflect how well your students can read and interpret information, and then present that information in a meaningful way. There are several presentation programs that are available on the market, and this might be a good time to teach your students how to use one or more of them. We like using KidPix™, PowerPoint™, PowerPix™, or HyperStudio™. They can then make multimedia reports and present them orally to a group of peers or another audience. Students can also use desktop publishing programs to create pamphlets, brochures, and calling cards. Microsoft Publisher™ and Adobe PageMaker™ are used by a lot of schools.

I always start out with something simple and build upon it. Listed below are some projects you can have your students complete. The lessons in this book can be adapted to follow any of these projects. Again, these are arranged from simple to difficult, to allow your students some success. You can also look at this list of projects and organize it for your students, based on their ability and capability on the Internet. That way, your students can be working on the same topic, but the outcome can be different.

HitList of Bookmarks or Favorites

- Select 2–5 bookmarks on a topic, and explain them in an oral report.

Top Ten List

- Collect the Ten Best Web Sites, or Ten Facts, or Ten Details about a Subject.

- Write the Top Ten List, and present to a group.

Reports

- Variations on the report writing theme: pen and paper, word processor, desktop publisher, electronic presentation program.

- Have students create a booklet, a pamphlet, or a brochure that follows definite guidelines. (Guidelines vary for each report—if you are doing a report on animals, students identify the animal of choice, draw/copy a picture of the animal, write about the animal's habitat, write about the animal's life cycle, write three facts about the animal, write about endangerment of the animal, bibliography, or references. See Chapters 8, 9 and 10 for sample reports.)

ABC Book

- Create an ABC book about a topic or theme, and present it to another class. (See Chapter 10 for a sample ABC book on Canada.)

Virtual Tour/Trip

- Select Web sites about a location (house, neighborhood, museum, city, state, country).

- Write about what you want to do there.

- Showcase the places to see and things to do while at the location. (See Chapter 11 for a virtual tour of Washington DC.)

Data Base

- Have your students write reports on subtopics of a theme, then collect Web sites for each subtopic. (See Chapter 8, *A Whale of a Time!*, for a sample matrix of a database project.)

Online Book Club or Literature Circle

- Have your students collaborate with another class on a particular topic. They can e-mail each other regularly to discuss the topic. This is a variation of a literature circle or a book club, where two classes are reading the same book and they write e-mail letters to each other about the theme, plot, characters, setting, and time of a particular story, book, piece of literature. (See Chapter 13, *Book in an Hour*, for a sample of a literature circle.)

WebQuest

- Give your students a problem to solve. (See Chapter 14, *Ambassador to Mexico WebQuest*, for a sample WebQuest lesson.)

Issues Report

- Search the Web and other resources on a particular issue.

Evaluation

The last step in the process is grading the product or project that your students have created. This too is a difficult part of the process, as these projects are not simple (even the easiest of them). They have several components, and students need to be accountable on all of them. The main components are listed below. Others are found at the end of each of the next eight chapters of the book.

First and foremost, students have to be evaluated on their product or project—the content and organization of the report. Next, evaluate their use of proper mechanics, such as spelling, syntax, semantics, form, and style. Next comes online efficiency—did they use their online time wisely and well? Next comes collaboration with others. Add other categories for your class as you see fit.

Each category is evaluated on a scale. The scale I like to use is Exemplary, Good, and Needs Improvement. Some teachers use a numerical scale where 5 is Outstanding, 3 is Average, and 1 is Not Acceptable. Decide which is best for you. Before you distribute the assignment to your students, write the rubric and give it to your students, so they can gauge their work. There are sample rubrics for each of the lessons that follow. Generally, I follow this type of procedure when developing a rubric.

Exemplary	Good	Needs Improvement
Start with this rank, and determine what the best paper will look like in each category.	The last rank to determine, as it is somewhere between exemplary and needs improvement.	After completing the exemplary rank, determine what the worst paper will look like in each category.

Teaching the Lesson

You have done the planning, you have a topic or theme that works for your students, and you have created the goal, rationale, objectives/outcomes, procedures and evaluation rubric. You have selected the product or project you want your students to work on, and you have designed some Internet logs to use to keep your students accountable and to help them create bibliographies or references lists. Now what do you do?

That's simple! Give a demonstration of what you want your students to do. Have a sample product or project ready for them to look at, and have it available for them to see throughout the lesson. Go over the evaluation rubric, so your students can plan ahead of time what they need to do to master the topic. Lastly, determine deadlines when the final product/project has to be completed, as well as some intermediate deadlines just to keep everyone on track.

You have it made! What follows are some sample lessons that follow these procedures. I hope you like them. Each of these lessons has been used and tested in hundreds of classrooms. Each works, but to make them work for you, you will need to modify them to fit you and your class. I hope you enjoy *The Online Classroom*. Please write to me at **cotton@instruction.com**, and tell me more about what you are doing in your classroom.

Ten Lesson-Planning Guidelines

As with managing your class, there are a few guidelines for planning effective Internet lessons. These, too, have been gleaned from many classrooms over the past few of years.

1. Develop a rationale or purpose as to why the lesson or unit is important and why it's important to use the Internet. This is important for both your students and their parents to know.

2. Create lessons that use a variety of resources, such as (offline) books, encyclopedias, dictionaries, journals and magazines, atlases, as well as the Internet. We are preparing these students for the future, where they will have to know many different ways to access information.

3. Have clear objectives for each unit of Internet-based instruction, and discuss them in detail with your students prior to starting. Give each student a copy of the objectives and lesson requirements right from the beginning.

4. Demonstrate the lesson to your class before they start to work online. This will clear up any confusion that might occur and reduce the amount of wasted online time.

5. Along the same lines, discuss each aspect of the lesson in detail, so your students know what to expect, and what they have to do, in order to learn the content.

6. Have your students develop a "Web site log," telling about the Web sites they have visited, and what they learned from them. Keep your students accountable, and keep them writing. Writing, as well as discussing and reflecting, are three keys to learning. A sample Web site log is included at the end of this chapter. To use the Web site log, the teacher needs to bookmark, or write on the board, three to five Web sites that the students are to visit during an Internet session.

7. Create lessons that scaffold one upon the other. Start out with easy lessons that let your students access one Web site. As your students gain experience and expertise, design more difficult lessons. Internet lessons are usually student-based, which means your kids will do them at their own pace. For greater success, start out easy and progress to lessons that require e-mail collaboration with other classes or electronic notebooks using PowerPoint™ PowerPix™, or HyperStudio™.

8. Bookmark three to five URLs for each lesson beforehand, so your students will have an idea of where they are expected to go on the Web.

9. Create specific worksheets or exercises for URLs to keep your students accountable.

10. Evaluation is important. Create rubrics that cover many facets of learning. Sample rubrics may be found at the end of each lesson in this book.

Web Site Log

Group Name: _____ Date: _____

Members: _____ _____

_____ _____

1. Copy the Web sites from the bookmark list (or the board) that deal with your topic:

http:// _____ Title: _____

http:// _____ Title: _____

http:// _____ Title: _____

http:// _____ Title: _____

http:// _____ Title: _____

2. Visit a Web site, and write its title: _____

_____

3. What was the main idea of the Web site? _____

_____

4. What are the four most important points of the Web site?

a) _____

b) _____

c) _____

d) _____

5. How are you going to use this information in your report?

_____

_____

_____

6. Repeat this procedure for three to five Web sites on your topic.

Internet Journal

Name _____ Date _____

Website Title: _____

URL: http:// _____

Write 3 facts about the website:

1. _____

2. _____

3. _____

Write how you will use the website in your report? _____

_____

Internet Log Questionnaire

Group Name _____ Date _____

Names of Members _____

What was the topic of the URLs you were reading today? _____

What did you learn from the URL that you did not know before? _____

_____

If you were showing the URL to someone else, how would you tell them about it?

_____

How will you use what you've learned today from the URL to improve your report?

_____

Section 2
Lessons

Chapter 7

E-pals & Keypals

The past few chapters have shown you ways to retrieve information from the Web using your browser. You have been visiting Web sites, reading information, clicking on links, and engaging in one-way communication. With e-mail (electronic mail) you can engage in two-way communication on the Internet, and you can initiate a conversation as well as reply to one. E-mail is one of the most powerful and useful tools available through the Internet. E-mail is also possibly the easiest service to use on the Internet.

When you're in an e-connection with your e-buddies around the world, snail-mail (a somewhat derogatory term for the postal system) becomes a thing of the past. No more phone tag, voice mail, missed calls, lost mail, insufficient postage, or expensive overnight FedExes. (Now we have downtime, system bugs, viruses, and the promise of upgrades instead!) With e-mail you are in direct, immediate, and almost instantaneous contact with people all around the world. (Some e-mail communications take time to get where they are going, depending on the technology involved; and even people who use e-mail still forget to read and answer their mail!) With e-mail, you can always find your corre-spondents, and they can always find you. You can write messages to each other, read messages, file them, print them out for docu-mentary evidence, and/or respond. And you can do all this with-out having to think on your feet as you do with a telephone call— you can take your time as you ponder your e-mail replies, correct them, or even change your mind and delete them rather than sending them. Then, once your messages are sent, many e-mail systems will automatically file away a copy of your reply for future reference. It's that simple and that wonderful!

Once you have an Internet account, you have an e-mail address. To send and receive e-mail, you need an e-mail software program. This is easy to solve as both Netscape and Internet Explorer have built in e-mail programs. Netscape calls their program Messenger, while the e-mail program for Internet Explorer is Outlook Express. In addition, there are so many stand alone e-mail programs on the market that I will not bother to attempt to list their names, discuss their merits, or explain how they work. They're all pretty much alike, except that the specific command language differs from program to program. For example, "write a message" in some programs might be called "compose" in other programs; in some programs, Command-S will send a message, while sending is accomplished with a Control-X command in other programs. And so on and so forth—you have to spend some time getting used to the quirks of whatever program you have. Most programs have more-or-less the same heading at the top of each message: a "To:" line (e-mail address of the recipient), a "Subject:" line (space for a topic heading), a "Copy:" or "cc:" line (if you want to send a copy of the message to someone else simultaneously), a bcc (for blind carbon copy so you can send the message to another person without the main "to" recipient being aware of it) and a "From:" line (your e-mail address to which your correspondent may reply); some programs are more complicated than this. Many Internet providers give you a copy of their preferred e-mail software, along with instructions.

Another item of similarity for all the programs is your unique address, yours alone, much like a social security number. E-mail addresses, while they might look long and somewhat confusing, are relatively easy to decode: Think of an e-mail address as analogous to a snail-mail address. In snail-mail, you have a name, a street address, a city, a state, and a ZIP code. Likewise with e-mail, you have a name, the @ sign, the server ID (= the street address), a dot (.), location of the server (= city and state), a dot (.), and a domain (= ZIP code).

One of my addresses is **ecotton@oavax.csuchico.edu—ecotton** in the "userid" area stands for Eileen Cotton, which is my name; the server is at (@) a computer called **oavax**, the server is located at

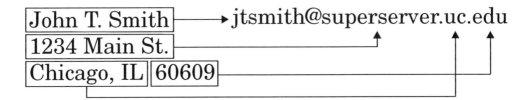

csuchico, which is short for California State University, Chico, where I teach, and it is in the educational or **.edu** domain. Quite often, the userid section is the first initial and last name of the person at that address, but this is not always true. I have an e-friend who has a series of numbers in the userid section of her address; while this makes her relatively anonymous, it is difficult to remember. Fortunately, many e-mail programs give you the ability to save e-mail addresses and give them nicknames so you don't need to remember long "handles."

Domains other than education (**.edu**) will be reflected in the last part of an e-mail address: **.com** (commercial); **.org** (nonprofit organization); **.k12** (school district); **.mil** (military); **.net** (network), and **.gov** (government). Some e-mail addresses will have a state and or country abbreviation in the domain area (the two-letter Post Office abbreviations are used): **.jp** for Japan; **.ca** for Canada; **.uk** for the United Kingdom; or **.nl** for the Netherlands. In the U.S., you might see a domain such as "**.in.us**" which means "Indiana, United States."

Have your students collect state and country domain codes from incoming e-mail. They can then locate the places on a map. This is similar to a stamp collection, only it's an e-mail country collection. See how many different states and countries are represented by the addresses they see on the Internet, then locate them on a world map. It's a painless way to learn geography. On the other hand, please do not encourage your students to randomly send e-mail messages to strangers in order to collect unusual addresses. This is not polite.

Notice that I have written my e-mail address in lowercase letters. Some ISPs give out "case sensitive" e-mail addresses. Therefore, if an e-mail address is written in upper and lower case letters and the system does not recognize upper case letters, you have a problem. Copy e-mail addresses exactly as they are sent or given to you. Do not change the case. If you do, you might receive a machine-generated reply like "Undeliverable Message" with no explanation as to why the message is undeliverable.

What purposes does being on e-mail serve? You can communicate with another person about a topic of interest to each of you, quickly and cheaply. You can share news, voice opinions, compare and contrast facts and figures. It's a great way to encourage your students to read and write in an "authentic" (real-life) situation.

It's electrifying for kids to realize that they are in e-contact with somebody in Russia or Africa or Asia. E-mail is fun, easy, informative, and inherently educative, for as they say, "travel is broadening," and e-mail is electronic travel. Now that we have e-mail, our telephone and mail habits have changed, as e-mail is the most-used portion of the Internet. Using e-mail will prepare your students for their immediate and future personal, academic, and business communications. E-mail also has the potential to improve reading, writing and spelling. I know of one school where the kids started to think about using proper grammar, something their teacher did not think was possible.

To communicate with someone else using e-mail, you need their e-mail address. At present, the best way to find someone's e-mail

address is to call them up and ask for it. Short of a phone call, you can try to find an e-mail address on the Web. At People Search (**http://people.yahoo.com/**) type in the first and last name of the person you are seeking. If you know the domain, type that in too. Click on return and if the person is registered, his or her e-mail address will show up on a list. I typed my name and my old e-mail address appeared. Therefore the information you receive might not be accurate. You can also find e-mail addresses at WhoWhere (**http://www.whowhere.lycos.com/**); The Internet Address Finder (**http://www.iaf.net/**), and WebCrawler's People Finder (**http://webcrawler.com/reference/email_lookup**). At AltaVista (**http://altavista.com**) click on People Finder; at Infoseek (**http://infoseek.go.com**) click on e-mail lookup. I looked my name up using all of the above "finders" and only Yahoo's People Finder found my e-mail address, but it was out of date. These search tools will only find folks if they are registered. Many people are not registering their e-mail addresses, just like folks have unlisted telephone numbers. If you are seeking people who are not registered, you will not be able to find their e-mail addresses.

Another way to find a specific address of someone you are seeking is to send an e-query to the "postmaster" or the "Webmaster" at the site where you think the person's e-mail account resides. People almost always include their e-mail address as part of the information on their home pages. If you forget my e-mail address, but remember my name, then either send a query to **postmaster@csuchico.edu** and ask for Eileen Cotton's address, or look me up on our CSU, Chico home page. Most postmasters and Webmasters are very helpful; some aren't though, sometimes for security reasons.

At first, you and your students may have the problem of having no one to send e-mail to. A quick and easy way to solve this problem is to subscribe to a list (often called a listserv)—a special-interest group that talks about something you are interested in. Right after you e-mail your subscription to the listserv—probably

that very day, and sometimes within minutes—you'll have more e-mail than you have time to read (fortunately, you can always delete messages that aren't of interest to you). After you have "lurked" on the sidelines for a while, learning the character of the list and the habits of the people who frequently post messages, you can take part by sending a message to the list. Your first message should be a simple one of self-introduction: "I'm new to this list. I'm interested in . . ." Someone will answer! You may be surprised at how many replies you will receive to your message. Here, however, is a point at which to teach your students reasonable cautiousness: Just as we tell kids not to take candy from strangers and not to get in cars with people they don't know, tell your kids not to give out their phone numbers, home addresses, credit-card numbers or other personal information over the Internet unless you or a parent knows.

How do you find lists that interest you and your students? How do you subscribe? These lists are sometimes called "mailing lists," "listservs" or "networks," and there are thousands of them. You can subscribe to lists that deal with kids, learning, education, computers, libraries, art, music, endangered species, media, sports, any content area you teach, and any subject you want.

To find up-to-date lists of mailing lists, go back to the Web and open Publicly Accessible Mailing Lists at **http:// www.neosoft.com/internet/paml/subjects/**. Click on a letter of the alphabet to see mailing list topics. At the same Web site, you can also find education-only mailing lists. Click on **http:// www.neosoft.com/internet/paml/subjects/education.html** and find a list of topics from lesson plans to attention deficit disorder. Another List of Lists, called TileNet, can be found at **http:// tile.net/lists/**. Each of these generic lists of lists will give you the basic information you need to both subscribe and unsubscribe. I will state again—mailing lists generate a lot of e-mail. Because of this, some schools do not allow students to subscribe.

E-Mail Etiquette or Netiquette

Before your kids start sending e-mail to friends or joining mailing lists, you have the perfect opportunity to teach a lesson on e-mail etiquette or "netiquette" as it is called. Just like you have to learn which fork to use when dining, there is a protocol to learn with e-

mail. It is impolite to write a message using UPPERCASE letters, as that seems like you are SHOUTING at your correspondent. Don't type any "naughty" words. Don't be overly antagonistic when you write a message; in other words, don't flame. The Netiquette Home Page by Arlene Rinaldi does a good job of explaining the proper rules of e-mail and the Internet. Go to **http://www.fau.edu/rinaldi/netiquette.html** and check it out. She claims she is not the "Miss Manners of the Internet," but she could have fooled me!

Deciding to Join a Mailing List

Given all the warnings, you decide to join a mailing list. In e-mailing your subscription to a listserv or mailing list, follow the directions for the mailing list carefully. When you decide to join a list, send your subscription to the correct e-mail address. Very quickly you will receive notice that your subscription has been received. Usually the Webmaster of the list will ask you to reply to the message within 24 or 48 hours if you want to be included on the list. If you do not respond to the message, you will not be included on the list. If you do respond, then the avalanche of e-mail will begin.

After you send your response to the list message, you will receive an e-mail stating the rules, protocols, and FAQs (frequently asked questions) of that list, among them being this most important question: "How do I get off this list?" Save this information! I didn't do that for the first two lists I subscribed to. Later, when I needed help, I did not know how to get it, and when I wanted to get off the lists, I didn't know how. Sometimes you want to take a vacation or escape from a list, and the set of FAQs tells you what you need to know to control the list's access to your e-mail box. Deleting the instructions is a terrible mistake! Either print-out the FAQs or save them to your hard drive so you can reference them easily.

All lists have three addresses: (1) the discussion address, for ordinary purposes; (2) the automatic address, for requests that will generate automatic machine-generated administrative responses; and (3) the address of the list moderator/owner/SysOp (systems operator). If you want to discuss things on the list, use the discussion address. If you want to unsubscribe, receive an archive of previous listings, find out who else is a member of the list, or get a digest version of today's correspondence, use the automatic address. If you want to talk privately to the moderator, use the third address. Try not to get these addresses confused. It is usually easier to remember the discussion address than it is to remember the other two. This is one of the few times when pencil and paper can still be helpful.

Use the moderator's personal address, not the listserv address, when you want to complain about some list member's lack of netiquette, or when you are hopelessly confused and don't know what to do next. The moderators of some lists look at the incoming mail and screen it for pertinence; other lists are unmoderated. For school purposes, I prefer moderated lists. A savvy, fair-minded moderator can keep a list civilized.

Lists just for kids abound, but since they generate a lot of e-mail, you need to think twice if you want your students to subscribe. There are a number of lists to which kids may subscribe and where they will find many willing penpals or, rather, keypals or e-pals. To subscribe to these lists, you and your students will send

subscription messages that follow the guidelines stated above. Click on E-Pals at **http:// www.epals.com/** and follow the directions on the page to register your class for an e-mail pal. Go to International E-mail Classroom Connections at **http://www.stolaf.edu/network/iecc/** for teachers who are seeking classes to partner with their classes for international and cross-cultural e-mail exchange. This list is maintained by St. Olaf's College. It is very comprehensive, and is one of the oldest and most reliable on the Web. Go to KeyPals at **http://www.mightymedia.com/keypals/**. They claim their Web site is the "safest way to connect . . . classroom to classroom . . . student to student . . . worldwide."

Other than setting up keypals and e-pals, what else can you do with e-mail? Lots! And a student of any age who can hunt and peck out words on a keyboard can take part. Even little kids who can't write or type can dictate messages to big kids who can. The idea of having e-mail waiting is very enticing, and most kids get excited at the discovery that there are people out there who want to speak with them. The ease with which one generates, corrects, and deletes text on an electronic keyboard; the relative interpersonal immediacy of e-mail; and all the many other fascinating aspects of this new toy, the computer on the Internet, make it the greatest incentive ever to early literacy. For little hands struggling to gain small-muscle control, it used to be hard to learn to write. Now it's easy—and they're never too young to start.

You can have your kids participate in e-mail projects. One that most kids seem to enjoy is The Monster Exchange at **http://www.win4edu.com/ minds-eye/monster/**. According to the Web page, "students try to communicate an original monster image into another child's mind using writing skills and technology." To see what the kids of Aberdeen, Washington and Cottonwood, Arizona did with this project, go to **http://www.techline.com/~tmallory/ monster/**. The Global School House has a Projects page at **http://www.gsn.org/project/index.html**. Here you can register for an online e-mail project. The E-mail Projects Home Page can be found at **http:// www.otan.dni.us/webfarm/emailproject/email.htm**. You'll see projects on writing, cookbooks (favorite foods), pizza (from my university no less), buying a house, home remedies, as well as other projects you might want to participate in.

One spring semester, I was in e-mail communication with a first-grade class, and the youngsters clearly understood what they were doing. Each week we talked about the flowers that were blooming and the birds that I had seen that past week. I would ask them mini-research questions and they would give me answers. Never think that your students are either too young or too sophisticated to participate. And don't be surprised or offended when your young students take more readily to computers and the Internet than you do. It's called the Generation Gap, and this time, you and I are on the wrong side! Turn them loose, let them go, and learn from them all you can!

In Your Classroom

Keypals on the Internet

Goal

To broaden the horizons of your students while encouraging reading and writing skills, higher-level thinking skills, and civilized discourse with other members of the human community.

Rationale

It's always nice to have someone else to talk to, to bounce ideas off of, and have a gossip fest with. It's also good to have friends all over the world in case you ever go on a long trip. More importantly, when we know people from other places, we tend to see our similarities, which might lead to greater world harmony.

Objective

Students write and respond once a week to a keypal not in their hometown. The purpose of the e-mail correspondence is to discuss, compare, contrast, and analyze topics that are being studied in class (from weather-watching to bird-watching, work and hobbies, culture and dating habits, moms and dads, food and algebra, world events and local disasters, just anything).

You must decide beforehand the exact purpose you want to emphasize, and you should have a class of e-mail recipients arranged which is also working on the same objective.

Procedure

Before starting this assignment, you have done the background search and identified a classroom of keypals for your students. Set the stage with your students by sharing some e-mail from a list on which someone from far away talks about a topic of interest to your class or, maybe, asks you a question about your students. Let your students choose from the keypals you have found. Make sure that everyone finds an e-pal, and that everyone gets a communication line started. As the semester progresses, prompt your students to engage their keypals in discussion of various aspects of topics and subjects being studied in your class.

Evaluation

By the end of the semester, your students will have gained a better understanding of, and broader perspectives on, the topics and subjects covered in your class because they will have absorbed the perspectives of their e-pals and keypals. They will have experienced reading the authentic writing of other people. They will have written their own ideas in cogent and meaningful ways that were efforts at being understood by respected peers, rather than just mere school exercises. They may have developed friendships that span miles and oceans and may stand the test of time.

Once your students have keypals, you and they can study geography by pinpointing the locations of e-mail correspondents. Suggest that your class make a "country collection" by looking at the domains at the end of each e-mail address. You can study language arts by looking at speech patterns, letter composition, spelling, and effective ways to convey an idea to other people. Your students are accustomed to having you correct their writing in terms of its content, cogency, organization, grammar, syntax, and spelling. Ask them, now, to pass judgment on the writing of their e-buddies—not that your students will necessarily remark to their e-pals and keypals on their English usage. If your class partners with a class of kids overseas learning to speak English, all of the students will have great fun learning English. As an added benefit, your students might learn another language too.

Another good e-mail project is the "Travel Bear." This takes a bit of time to set up, but the rewards are great. You need to arrange a set of classes where you can virtually send your "travel bear." On allotted days, when the "travel bear" arrives at a particular class, that class takes him on a tour of the town and writes an adventure for the travel bear. The tour and the account of the adventure gets sent to all the classes in the travel loop. By the time the "travel bear" comes home from his trip, he has visited with several different classes, maybe in different countries, and he has a story from each place. These stories can then be published in your classroom and read by everyone. Also, you can follow up on the stories by writing to the classes in the travel loop, asking questions and finding out more details, as well as tracing his route on a map. It's a lot of fun to see where the travel bear is going next! See Journey Bear Down Under at **http:// www.fsd38.ab.ca/Schools/Spitzee/jbear2.htm** to see what a class in Canada did with this project.

Since I work with a lot of classes, I find that each time we do an e-mail project we need to have some definite guidelines, or the conversation will wither. Develop a worksheet that lets your students write the e-mail message before they send it. Have a buddy check the e-mail message for any kind of errors. Then, have the students type the e-mail message before sending it online. Keep track of these drafts, as it keeps your students accountable. Of course, writing and proofreading practice are always useful.

In addition, if you are doing an ongoing e-mail project, have students keep a log of whom they are writing including name and e-mail address, topic, letter and response. It's a diary that tells where they have been and what they have been doing. It's a good way for your students to keep track of the conversation too.

You have to maintain your interest in e-mail in order to keep a project ongoing. Therefore, post a weekly topic for e-mail discussion and have your students write at least one letter on that topic to their e-pal. At the end of the week, discuss what your students have found out about that topic. Think about topics that your students would like to discuss and use them. I also like to take a topic that shows up in the headlines and use that as a point of discussion. When you get several classes across several states talking about one topic, your students learn to see the value of looking at an idea from different perspectives.

The last and maybe most important aspect about e-mail is its uncanny ability to level the playing field. With e-mail you do not have any prejudices. You do not know who is writing to you, you have no idea about color or race. You are just writing an e-mail message to someone and someone is responding to you. This can go on for many, many letters before you find out that this person is "green with pink spots" and you are not supposed to like green people with pink spots . . . but by then it's too late, as you do like that person. Because you do not know anything about the sender of an e-mail message, stay on "approved" penpal and e-mail project Web sites. Also, do not have your students use their full name when participating in e-mail projects. "JA from the 4th grade" is enough of a description.

You and your class can engage in cross-cultural communication, explore others' points of view, learn about distant countries, and expand your minds and hearts to awareness of other people's holidays, celebrations, clothing styles, food, hobbies, hopes, and loves. Your kids will be fascinated to find out the similarities and differences of other kids' lives, their parents and siblings, who lives in the household, and what other kids do for spending money. Try communicating with a class in a different time zone or hemisphere. They might learn why time zones are important and why the seasons are different in different parts of the world.

The number and styles of lessons you can do involving e-mail are limited only by your own and your students' imaginations. Use e-mail and list participation at all grade levels. Let your lesson-planning creative juices flow, and you and your students will discover that your own classroom is the center of the universe.

Chapter 8:
A Whale of a Time!

Marine mammals fascinate kids. They want to give the creatures humanlike qualities and characteristics because these mammals "look intelligent" and have a language of their own. Kids feel the need to both communicate with these amazing creatures as well as save them from harm. So they want to "Free Willy" and swim with Flipper.

There are many Web sites devoted to whales, dolphins, seals, sea lions, elephant seals, sea otters, polar bears, walruses, manatees, and the other marine mammals. This chapter contains a lesson to help you refine your Internet techniques, while simultaneously teaching about these remarkable marine mammals.

The learning plan I'm using in this book can be summed up as "both at the same time." I offer you a way to teach both content and method, both subject matter and Internet skills at the same time. Learn all about marine mammals while learning how to become a better Web-walker.

If you want to, review Chapter 1 to remind yourself of the basics of the Web and how your browser functions. Revisit the searching exercises proposed in Chapter 3, but this time search for "whale" and "marine mammal." How many hits did you get? This should give you a good start. Listed below is a lesson with relevant URLs that will let you carry your whaling a bit further.

☘ In Your Classroom

Marine Mammal Database

Goal

To develop a better understanding of the characteristics, habitats, and aquatic adaptations of marine mammals, while furthering your understanding of your Web browser.

Rationale

Many kids think that marine mammals are among some of the world's most interesting creatures. They are among the largest animals on earth, and their lives are full of contradictions. They live in the ocean yet they breathe air. They communicate quite effectively using tweets, whistles, clicks, grunts, moans, and other sounds that reverberate through both air and water, yet we cannot understand them. They look and swim like fish, yet they are not fish. Marine mammals might be a window on what makes "man" human, and "animal" not human.

As your students learn about marine mammals, their habitats, and how they communicate with one another, include in your lesson plan the attempts humans have made to communicate with marine mammals and to save them from extinction. Have them imagine what the world would be like if these magnificent mammals were extinct.

Objectives

- Students will search the Web for information on marine mammals.

- Students will create a database highlighting habitat, characteristics, life span, pictures, and literature/ writing/books/stories about marine mammals.

- Students will discuss similarities and differences among the various types of marine mammals.

- Students will explain the ways humans have tried to protect marine mammals from extinction.

- Students will create a report to deliver the information to classmates.

Procedures

Set the stage by showing pictures of marine mammals to heighten your students' interest. Brainstorm with your students about what they already know about marine mammals, using a K-W-L chart like the one pictured below:

K-W-L about Marine Mammals		
What do I **KNOW** about Marine Mammals?	What do I **WANT** to know about Marine Mammals?	What have I **LEARNED** about Marine Mammals?

Make at least two versions of the K-W-L Chart: a larger master chart to hang in your classroom and a smaller one for each group of students. During the first session, your students will fill in the first two columns of the master chart. As it fills up with information, everyone can see exactly what they are learning.

Using the big K-W-L chart as a guide, have your students develop their own K-W-L charts for a marine mammal that particularly interests them. They can choose from a wide variety of fields of information, including—but not limited to—the following: habitat; characteristics of a particular species; characteristics of individual marine mammals; pictures of marine mammals; impact of the Marine Mammal Protection Act on specific groups and habitats; various marine mammals in stories, books, and poetry; scientific articles and reports about marine mammals;

communication techniques of various species; human attempts to communicate with marine mammals; and, human uses of marine mammals hunting and harvesting.

After your students have completed gathering their information and developing their group K-W-L charts, these charts form the basis for creating a report to the class on the marine mammal(s) they have learned more about. This report can involve the creation of a Web site, a closed-circuit television production, a panel debate, or an oral report. From the K-W-L charts a comparison/contrast chart can be developed to show similarities and differences among the various marine mammals.

From all the information gathering and presentations, a class database can be amassed on marine mammals, making the collected information readily accessible. Using a database program, such as "Claris Works" or "Microsoft Works," key the charted information in the various categories, where it can be easily revised, expanded, corrected, and reformatted. A sample Marine Mammal Database is found at the end of the chapter. This database can then be transferred to a set of Web pages that can be used for future reference, not only by your class, but by others. The database also becomes a substantial basis for filling in the third column on the big K-W-L chart: "What we LEARNED."

Evaluation

The several individual and group K-W-L charts, and the in-class presentations made in reference to them, form one basis of assessment. Look at the sample evaluation rubric for this lesson (at the end of the chapter), and notice that it focuses on four areas: Content, Internet Experience, Mechanics and Cooperation.

Use the big K-W-L chart as a class equalizer, having made sure that everyone took part in contributing to the big chart. Collaborative effort ought to result in greater results than merely individual effort. Make sure that it does!

This unit on marine mammals may be the first solo Web-walking that your students have done. Help them get started, if they have trouble. To help you get started, check out the URLs below. In fact, you might want to set up the bookmarks on your browser to include these Web sites.

"A Full Net"

⦿ Whales: A Thematic Web Unit

http://curry.edschool.Virginia.EDU/go/Whales/

From the University of Virginia, this is an Internet-based thematic unit of study that spans several areas of the curricula, each focusing on whales.

⦿ The Virtual Whale Project

http://fas.sfu.ca/cs/research/Whales/

A three-dimensional Web site environment with animation and sound, developed to showcase the feeding behaviors of Pacific Humpback whales.

⦿ Discovering Whales

http://whales.magna.com.au/DISCOVER/index.html

This page is part of the "Welcome to the World of Watery Whales" page. It contains links to some of the 77 species of cetaceans living in the ocean. Scroll down a bit before you find the list of whales. Be patient, the information is good.

⦿ The Whale Times

http://www.whaletimes.org/whahmpg.htm

This is a newspaper for kids that has facts and pictures about whales and sharks.

⦿ The Whale Information Network

http://www.webmedia.com.au/whales/whales6.html

An Australian Web site that has whale facts, whale history, and plenty more.

⦿ The Sperm Whale Project

http://www.alaska.net/~pratt/programs/spermwhale/

Find out what happens when a dead sperm whale washes ashore in Alaska.

⦿ The Whale Watcher Expert System

http://vvv.com/ai/demos/whale.html

At this Web site, you can learn how to identify different varieties of whales.

⦿ Vancouver Aquarium Science Center AquaFacts

http://oceanlink.island.net/vanaqu.html

The folks at Vancouver Aquarium Science Center (B.C., Canada) have developed a Web site for kids to find out facts about gray whales, killer whales, dolphins and porpoises, beluga whales, as well as other marine animals.

⦿ The California Gray Whale Tutorial

http://198.188.248.11/whale/whale1.html

A great Web site to learn all there is to know about the California Gray Whale. The page is maintained by San Luis Obispo County public schools in California. SLO, CA (as it is called) is right along the Pacific coast and these folks get a good view of the Gray Whale migration each year.

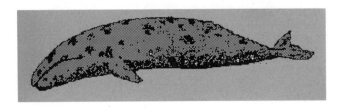

⬤ Sea World Marine Mammals

http://www.seaworld.org/infobook.html

You can find a list of links to many marine mammals at this site. The information is geared to kids. Each of these sites has links about physical characteristics, scientific classification, habitat, food and feeding, gestation, sleep, and social structure, for particular marine mammals. A few links are listed below:

Baleen Whales
http://www.seaworld.org/baleen_whales/ baleen_whales.html

Beluga Whales
http://www.seaworld.org/beluga_whales/befirst.html

Bottlenose Dolphins
http://www.seaworld.org/bottlenose_dolphin/ bottlenose_dolphins.html

Harbor Seals
http://www.seaworld.org/HarborSeal/hsintro.html

Killer Whales
http://www.seaworld.org/ killer_whale/killerwhales.html

Manatees
http://www.seaworld.org/manatee/ manatees.html

Walruses
http://www.seaworld.org/walrus/ walrus.html

⬤ Careers in Marine Science

http://www.rtis.com/nat/user/elsberry/marspec/ mmstrat.html

If you have students who want to become marine biologists, this is the Web site for them.

○ American Cetacean Society Factsheet

http://www.acsonline.org/factshts.htm

Click on this page and find out information on the bowhead, blue, fin, gray, humpback, and sperm whale, and the bottlenose and common dolphin. There is also a set of diagrams on the parts of whale.

○ Bill Lemus' List of Links

http://www.rtis.com/nat/user/elsberry/marspec/ms_blem.html

Considered one of the best sources of Web information on marine mammals with too many Web sites to count. The Web site is in alphabetical order, so you can speed through it if you know what you are looking for. Many of the links have marine mammal pictures as well as text.

○ Canadian Arctic Profiles: Species

http://www.schoolnet.ca/collections/arctic/species/species.htm

Part of the great School Net pages developed in Canada. Click on this page and scroll down to find link on seals, walruses, baleen whales and toothed whales. The information is ready for kids to use.

○ The Mediterranean Monk Seal

http://www.weburbia.com/pg/seal.htm

Information and resources on the monk seal.

○ Charlotte, The Vermont Whale

http://www.uvm.edu/whale/whalehome.html

In 1849 the bones of a mysterious creature were found in Charlotte, Vermont. The bones were from a fossilized whale skeleton. Information about this ancient whale is at this Web site.

○ The Great Whales

http://explorer.scrtec.org/explorer/
explorer-db/html/783750390-447DED81.html

A (Mac only) hypercard stack you can download that contains information about every type of whale known to humanity.

○ Marine Mammal Protection Act

http://www4.law.cornell.edu/uscode/16/ch31.html
(the 1972 law)
http://www.cnie.org/nle/biodv-11.html
(the 1994 amendment to the MMPA)

This is the Marine Mammal Protection Act as it is written in law. It is not easy to read, but if you have students researching the law, it is an important Web site .

○ The Wild Dolphin Project

http://wwwa.com/dolphin/index.html

An information source for the Atlantic Spotted Dolphin.

⬤ The Polar Bear and the Walrus

http://www.teelfamily.com/activities/polarbear/

A Web page written for homeschoolers to learn more about these two marine mammals.

⬤ Killer Whale Sounds

http://www.killerwhale.org/sounds.html

At this page you can listen to some of the 62 different sounds made by the killer whale. You might need to download special plug-ins. The Web page is part of the British Columbia Wild Killer Whale Adoption Project. It's an interesting Web site at **http://www.killerwhale.org/index.html**.

Teaching resources for teachers, Learning resources for students

Many ready-made lesson plans about marine mammals are downloadable from the Internet for your immediate classroom use. You and your students can find them at these URLs:

Studying Whales in Middle Schools

⬤ SWIMS: Studying Whales in Middle School

http://www.ssec.org/idis/cohasset/TblCnt.htm

A constructivist lesson that lets students explore a question as if they were scientists. This is an integrated unit of study that is fun to use.

⬤ All About Seals, Sea Lions and Walruses

http://www.seaworld.org/Pinnipeds/introduction.html

This is a K–3 teacher's guide to a hands-on lesson that the folks at Sea World have developed so your students can learn more about these animals and the ecology of the ocean. The lessons integrate science, math, art, language and geography.

● WhaleNet "Blubber Glove" Activity Curriculum Unit

http://whale.wheelock.edu/whalenet-stuff/
Blubberglove.html

Have your students make a "blubber glove" to discover how blubber really works.

Pick Your Animal!

Now you know what the Web can do for you as a teacher, but only on one narrow range of topics: marine mammals. The world is a zoo, and we are but a few of the critters in it. Use the search engines, adapt the learning strategies suggested here, pick your own favorite critter and let your students pick theirs. Then Web-walk bravely to discover further information and more activities, instructional ideas and strategies that suit your style of teaching and your students' inclinations. All you have to do is click on your favorite search engine or directory to find Web pages about Ornithology, Farm Animals, Amphibia, and the like. Search for "Zoo Animal" or "African Animal" if you want a place to get started (remember not to search for plural words as it confuses the search engine). You'll be amazed at how many different creatures inhabit our world, and how much you can find out about them on the Internet. This must be what they meant when they said: "Learning is fun."

Sample Marine Mammal Database

Marine Mammal	Picture	Habitat	Life Span	Books/Stories	Diet	Characteristics
Baleen Whale						
Blue Whale						
CA Grey Whale						
Humpback Whale						
Right Whale						
Toothed Whale						
Killer Whale						
Minke Whale						
Pilot Whale						
Sperm Whale						
Dolphins						
Atlantic Dolphin						
Bottlenose Dolphin						
Spotted Dolphin						
Seals & Sea Lions						
Elephant Seal						
Harp Seal						
Sea Lion						
Dugong						
Manatee						
Polar Bear						
Sea Otter						
Walrus						

This database can be made into a Web page. By clicking anywhere on the matrix, you can find information about each of the marine mammals listed. Please note that this is not an exhaustive database on marine mammals!

Evaluation Rubric for "A Whale of a Time!"

Assessment Area	Exemplary	Proficient	Not Yet
Content	• Detailed & interesting information • Personal insights included • Relevant to students • Well written report • Positive addition to the database • Creativity shows in report • Shows initiative • Clear ideas • Well organized	• Less detail • Added database information • Completed KWL • Followed directions • Ideas less clear • Some detail, but organization wanders	• Not detailed • Did not complete database or KWL • Did not participate with others • Did not follow directions • Unclear ideas • Unorganized and boring
Internet Experience	• Searched many useful Web sites • Used traditional and electronic research tools • Used e-mail, listservs and newsgroups to find information • Wrote HTML for database	• Searched limited number of Web sites and traditional resources • Limited bibliography	• Searched one Web site • Only used one type of information source
Mechanics	• Excellent grammar, punctuation • Report is easy to read and follow	• Good grammar, punctuation and spelling • Errors do not "get in the way" of the story line	• Faulty grammar, punctuation and spelling • Report is difficult to read because of errors
Cooperation	• Students worked well together • Students shared the work load fairly • Students solved problems in a fair manner	• Students worked together with little strife • Burden of work done by small part of the group • Students solved most problems in a fair manner	• Students did not work well together • Burden of work done by one member of the group • Teacher intervention was needed to solve problems

Chapter 9:
The CyberNews

I
t's hard for some kids to become interested in state, national, and international news or current events. They do not yet grasp how world events effect their daily lives. Their sense of caring about people they do not know personally has not developed. Kohlberg and Piaget would say their processes of moral development are incomplete. Another cause of students' lack of connection with a world bigger than their own wants and needs is that the network news programs do not attempt to reach young people. The advertisers aim at selling their products to older folk—they know who's watching. The news on PBS is all talking heads, slow-moving, and cerebral; the news on the commercial networks is more colorful, more active, and with more human interest, but little is offered to attract the attention of anyone still in school.

So I started thinking about how to make the news less boring and encourage kids to become better informed by including the Internet in the equation. The Internet offers action and color like a television broadcast, but—unlike TV—the Internet is not a passive medium. The Internet activates the brain, while TV dulls it. Hands-on Web-walkers don't just sit there and watch; they interact.

ZoneMedia

I started thinking that there is more to news than just politics or street violence. There is Sports, which can be accessed through a multitude of sites on the Internet, such as ESPN SportsZone (**http://espn.go.com/dist/m/**

index.html) or Fox Sports at **http://foxsports.com** or Sports at **http://sports.excite.com**. I believe in trying almost anything to get my students hooked on the news, be it sports, human interest, ecology, wars, crises, elections, or whatever. Current events are important, so I pull out all the stops to prove that news is interesting. The Internet can help, because with it, students can make their own news. What could be better than personal attention.

The Internet is up-to-date because news on the Internet comes in real time. People who spend lots of time online regularly exploit the Internet for its news-gathering potential. Not only can you tap the usual resources such as CNN (**http://www.cnn.com**) or MSNBC (**http://www.msnbc.com/**), you can also quickly find information from less commercial sources such as e-mail, lists, and newsgroups.

In class, you can use the Web to access the news on the Internet. Yahoo News (**http://www.yahoo.com/headlines/**) has headline news updated regularly. You can read the AP Wire at **http://www1.trib.com/NEWS/APwire.html**. It is regularly updated. You can make news-gathering a daily part of your curriculum; you can build a news perspective into any thematic unit that you teach; and, you can make learning how to find the news, read the news, and understand the news as part of your instructional learning via the Internet. Once they get hooked, you will have created a few more news junkies, but that's the risk you run.

🍎 In Your Classroom

Read the CyberNews!

One way to get your students involved with the news is to have them regularly publish their own CyberNews or stage their own news broadcasts. If you want them to work on reading and writing skills, set up a news publishing organization in your classroom. If you want them to work on oral communication skills, have them produce and perform CyberNews broadcasts. They can practice their presentation skills using PowerPoint™ and HyperStudio™ authoring programs. At the stage when they use the Internet for news-reading, news-gathering, news-understanding, and news-summarizing, the process is essentially the same, whether ultimately they will present their results in print, in person, or online.

To set up your CyberNews Bureau (CNB), brainstorm with your students about the various departments or areas they will cover. Local, state, national, and international news departments come to mind, but you might want to have specialized departments such as sports, music, fashion, comics, gossip, weather, lifestyle, food, and human interest. This is also a chance to include an editorial department, featured columnists/commentators, and even letters to the editor from the readers.

Divide the class into teams of Internet reporters, one team for each major department. Their tasks are to find items from the various news sources; Internet as well as traditional print and video variety. They need to understand and interpret what they find, and then report (write) their own news stories. (Whether they produce a newspaper or a broadcast, they still need to write copy.)

The means of publication are up to you, your students, and the technical capabilities at your disposal. Your class could sponsor a weekly news broadcast over the school's P.A. system. If you have closed-circuit TV in your school, you could prepare a TV news program for broadcast regularly (once a month). You could publish your class' own newspaper for distribution to school mates, parents, and neighbors. You can have teams make PowerPoint presentations or HyperStudio stacks for each other. You can print a CyberNewspaper, or put it on the Web electronically. The possibilities are endless!

Goals

- To gain a better understanding of current events, their local and global impact.

- To learn how news is gathered and prepared for release to the public.

- To learn how to produce a newspaper or a news broadcast.

- To learn personal, intellectual responsibility in communicating matters of import to other fellow human beings.

Rationale

Young people need to know that they are not isolated but part of a larger sphere of interest and influence that encompasses the world. By expanding their horizons, they will learn to think about how local, state, national, and international events all work together to "make the world go around."

Objectives

- Students will read and gather news stories from traditional and Internet sources for the purposes of reporting this information to the class.

- Students will write articles based on the news they have gathered.

- Students will publish the news in a format that has been selected as best for the class.

- Students will maintain their CyberNewspaper on a regular basis either by publishing new editions or updating the CyberNews Web page for the class.

Procedures

Whet your students' appetites for news by asking them what events of the last week really caught their attention or sparked their imagination. Discuss those items and then list them on the board or monitor so that they look like the headlines of a newspaper. Tell your students that for the next semester (or however long you want the unit to last), they are going to be reporters and news anchors, working on the school news. They will be telling the main events of the week in some of the categories previously listed and offering their editorial opinion on the news they are presenting, following the cues found in network news programs or in Web-based news pages.

Explore the various news resources available to them—newspapers, news magazines, radio, television, and the Internet—not to forget their own personal reporting of the local news. Have your class divide itself up according to individual interests into the various news departments.

To create a CyberNewspaper to put on the Web, you will need a staff of people who can do the following:

- Editors who are responsible for topics that need to be researched for the CyberNews. Editors are responsible for timelines and deadlines on stories.

- Reporters who are responsible for researching the topics and writing the stories before the deadline. They are responsible for seeking related Web sites to enhance each article in the CyberNews.

- Co-editors who are responsible for researching the topics and editing the stories for accuracy of facts and grammar. Once the stories have been edited, they need to be rewritten by either the reporters or the co-editors.

- Artists who are responsible for creating or finding artwork that fits the edited stories.

- Layout designers who are responsible for the "look" of the CyberNews. They are the people who decide background color for a Web page and positioning of graphics and other artwork.

If you are going to put your editions of CyberNews on the Web, then you will need the following:

- Coders who are responsible for HTML coding the edited stories.

- Proofers who are responsible for proofreading the HTML coding for errors and correcting the errors.

- Webmasters who are responsible for submitting the CyberNewspaper to your local Internet Service Provider (and/or to Discovery Channel School if you wish). They are responsible for reporting on how well the CyberNews Team collaborated.

Evaluation

The newspaper or broadcast that your students produce will be the tangible result of this learning process. There is a CyberNews Rubric included at the end of this chapter that looks at the following topics: ideas and content; organization; mechanics; arts/graphics; and, cooperation. In the long run, look to see if your students have learned something about current events and whether they can carry on an interesting and informed conversation about the realities around them.

I do not take up space in this book listing the various major newspapers, news magazines, and radio and television sources. You and your kids have TVs and radios; turn them on to find out what's there; go to the newsstands to see what they offer. Nor do I take up space talking about what to do with your news, once you get it. You may decide to publish a newspaper or broadcast the news. If you do, I hope you take advantage of any number of good books, teacher's guides, and periodical literature on journalism and broadcasting. These can give you ideas on how to address your public and the technology of your chosen medium. I hope that you will decide to post your CyberNews to the Internet. If you do take that route, I enter herewith my subscription to your news service: cotton@instruction.com. Thanks!

CyberNewspaper Resources

◉ CRAYON

http://crayon.net/

Although it does not sound like a newspaper, it is. CRAYON is an acronym (of sorts) that stands for CReAte Your Own Newspaper. CRAYON offers supercool methods of styling your own headlines, as well as links in the following categories: U.S. News, Regional and Local News, World News, Politics As Usual, Editorials and Opinions, Weather Conditions and Forecasts, Business Reports, Information and Technology Report, Arts and Entertainment, Sports Day, The Funny Pages, and New and Cool Web Sites. CRAYON is an excellent site to learn how to make a newspaper work, a must-see for your students, and a good jumping-off place to find out more information for each of the departments that might be included in your own newspaper.

Newspaper Links

● The University of Florida, College of Journalism and Communications

http://www.jou.ufl.edu/commres/webjou.htm

This list of links to commercial newspapers with Web editions all over the world is rich and extensive.

● NandO Times

http://www.nandotimes.com/

This site has links to Global News, Stateside News, Sports, Politics, Business,

Information Technology, Health and Science, Entertainment, Jobs/Classified Ads, and Editorials.

● Current World News

http://www.yahoo.com/headlines/international/

Yahoo provides a summary of international headlines and stories with regular updates.

The New York *Times* at **http://www.nytimes.com/**, The San Francisco *Chronicle and Examiner* at **http://www.sfgate.com/** and *USA Today* at **http://www.usatoday.com/** all have online editions. In addition, most search tools have a headline news component. Check out AltaVista (**http://altavista.com**), WebCrawler (**http://www.webcrawler.com**), Cyber 411 (**http://209.116.217.64/**), Excite (**http://www.excite.com/**) and PlanetSearch (**http://www.planetsearch.com/**) to name a few.

Sports News on the Net

◉ NandO Sport Server

http://www2.nando.net/SportServer/

This Web site has links to football, baseball, hockey, basketball, and other sports.

◉ The Sporting News

http://www.sportingnews.com/

Find out the latest sports new for each of the leagues as well as auto racing, golf and more. A very comprehensive page that is sited as the source for other online sports information.

◉ The World Wide Web Virtual Library

http://www.justwright.com/sports/

A British Web site that features a built-in search engine, and links to many sports. Sports aficionados will never want to stop reading this book of electronic pages.

◉ WebCrawler Sports

http://www.webcrawler.com/sports/

Many search tools have a sports component. This is the sports page found at WebCrawler. Yahoo Sports is at **http://sports.yahoo.com/**.

American Government

⬤ Thomas: The U.S. Congress on the Net

http://thomas.loc.gov/

This Web site (named for Thomas Jefferson) has links to the House, the Senate,

the Congressional Record, the Library of Congress, and many other departments that focus on politics and American life.

National Weather Service forecasts

⬤ USA Today Weather

http://www.usatoday.com/weather/wfront.htm

See a copy of the USA Today weather map as well as forecasts for any region in the U.S.

⬤ The Weather Underground

http://www.wunderground.com/

Similar to USA Today and you can set the heat index for each area of the country too.

⬤ University of Illinois, Urbana Campus

http://www.uiuc.edu/misc/weather.html

For U.S. weather maps, as well as forecasts for every state in the union, this is the Web site to visit. You will find links to the latest weather image of the U.S., current weather maps, weather movies, and a link to current earthquakes (**http:// quake.usgs.gov/QUAKES/CURRENT/current.html**).

I did not mention news magazines on the Web, because there are so many. However, check out Pathfinder at **http:// pathfinder.com/welcome/** which has links to *Time* and *People* magazines, as well as links to sports, the stock market, travel, kidstuff, music, games, and more.

As you and your students work with the news, you will find many more resources and locations than I have offered here. In my experience, getting kids to become news reporters is one of the best ways to get them to have fun while learning, and to learn something useful while they are having fun.

Evaluation Rubric for "The CyberNews"

Assessment Area	Exemplary	Proficient	Not Yet
Ideas and Content	• Ideas are clear • Lots of details • Holds attention	• Ideas somewhat clear • Some details • Reader can follow most of story	• Unclear ideas • Details are too general and vague • Boring
Organization	• Very good introduction • Smooth, easy pace • Good placement of details • Strong conclusion	• Good introduction • Some trouble following pace • Some details, but out of order • Good conclusion	• Introduction boring • Hard to read • Wanders aimlessly • Stops abruptly or drags on
Art/Graphics	• Reflects research • Follows a plan • Carefully and neatly done • Art/graphics are an asset to the text	• Reflects some research • Shows some planning • Mostly done carefully and neatly • Art/graphics aid the text	• Does not reflect research • Is not planned • Is not done carefully and neatly • Art/graphics harmful to text
Internet Experience	• Used many Web sites to collect news • Daily Web site log entries • Related Web site news to print news in meaningful ways • Published product (Web site) is organized and easy to use • Updates on published product (Web site) occur every week	• Used required Web sites • Web site log entries 3–4 times a week • Used only news from either Internet or traditional media • Published product (Web site) is complicated to use • Updates on published product (Web site) occur once a month	• Used fewer than required Web sites • Web site log entries fewer than 2 times a week • Used news from only one source • Published product (Web site) is incomplete • Updates on published product (Web site) do not occur
Mechanics	• Excellent grammar, punctuation and spelling • Easy to read aloud	• Good grammar, punctuation and spelling • Most parts are easy to read	• Faulty grammar, punctuation and spelling • Awkward to read out loud
Cooperation	• Students worked well together • Students shared the work load fairly • Students solved problems in a fair manner	• Students worked together with little strife • Burden of work done by small part of the group • Students solved most problems in a fair manner	• Students did not work well together • Burden of work done by one member of the group • Teacher intervention was needed to solve problems

Chapter 10:
The ABCs
of Canada

A is for Archie, B is for Browser, C is for Computer . . . Alphabet books are among the first texts that little people read, yet they are developed by big people. The idea behind this lesson is for older kids to use the Internet to make an alphabet book for younger kids, and not one based on computer jargon, either.

The chosen topic can represent just about anything, so long as it is broad enough to offer words aplenty to use up the alphabet. An easy ABC book would be on animals. The older kids would already be inclined to start with Aardvark and end with Zebra. The challenge to them is finding information about these critters on the Web. Once they have finished their work, you can arrange for a cross-grade collaboration between, say, your upper graders and the lower graders down the hall or at another school. Sit a couple of older kids and a couple of younger kids in front of the same computer, and let the older kids show the younger kids their bestiary abecedarium, and then let the older kids and younger kids walk the Web together in search of a zoo-full of more animals. The upper graders could teach the lower graders how to browse, and the lower graders could demonstrate what they already know and more.

ABC books are relatively easy to think about if we deal with topics we know a fair amount about already. I want to focus on a topic that might be more difficult, or at least less familiar: Let's make an "Online ABC Book of Canada."

Canada, our neighbor to the north, is studied during both middle-school and high-school years, but American study of Canada tends to be inadequate, at best. Most Canadians with a high-school education know infinitely more about the USA than their American counterparts know about Canada. Most Americans don't know, for example, that the U.S. attempted to conquer and annex Canada in 1812, but failed, being beaten back by the Canadians at the Battle of Queenstown Heights. Canadians, you may be sure, know this! And this is only the beginning of American ignorance about "the True North" (as some Canadians call their land). After the typically inadequate study of Canada by American school kids, they still often don't know that Canada is the largest country (in terms of land mass) in the world, yet with a total population smaller than that of California. Most of us don't know that Canada is divided into provinces and territories. We cannot name them, nor locate them on a map. Most of us don't know that the United States and Canada share one of the longest open, unguarded borders in the world. Only the American tourist to Canada finds out that Canada does not have a dollar bill but a dollar coin, nicknamed "the Loonie." If your students do not yet know this kind of information about our fascinating northern friends and relatives—or about French-speaking Quebec, or the very many Canadian Native North Americans, or the recent migration to Canada of Ukrainians, Hong Kong Chinese, and several other nationalities that help to make up the complex and delightful Canadian national and ethnic mosaic (Canadians speak about a "mosaic" in preference to the American metaphor of a "melting pot")—then it's time to walk the Web to find out about Canada.

✎ In Your Classroom

The ABC Book of Canada

Goals

- To gain a better understanding of Canadians, their land, geography, and government; their culture, history, and ethnic heritage; and their feelings about Americans.

- To begin the assembly of a body of information that will allow students to compare American culture with another culture.

- To examine a culture similar enough to make the comparison interesting, and yet different enough to make us examine why we are what we are and they are what they are.

Rationale

The Land of the Maple Leaf is America's largest and most important trading partner. One of the two official languages of Canada is English; this means that Americans can speak their own tongue and be understood almost anywhere they go in Canada. Canada is one country to which Americans are likely to travel because it is easier than going to any other foreign country (if Canada is "foreign"). Part of the fun of studying Canada is finding out the ways in which they are "just like us" and the ways in which they are "really different." Because Canada is part of the course of study in U.S. schools, let's use the Internet to help us do a better job of finding out about our cousins to the north. Walk the Web and take a Canadian vacation without leaving home.

Objectives

- Students will gather information about Canada using both online and offline resources.

- Students will compare and contrast Canadian culture with American culture.

- Students will study maps, charts, flags, pictures, and text to collect information about Canada.

- Teams of students will compose an ABC book of Canada to share with another class of students.

Procedures

Set the stage by reading an ABC book to your class and letting them talk about the ABC books that they had "back when they were children." Hold a discussion about the elements of an ABC book. Propose making an ABC book that can be shared with another class. Talk about Canada, activating your students' prior knowledge about Canada and proposing that Canada be the topic of the ABC book. Using the suggestions below, as well as whatever your students themselves find on their own, explore the Internet for information about Canada, relating this to any other information about Canada available from other sources.

Because there is so much about Canada on the Internet, an important part of this lesson will be learning to discriminate among sources: avoiding redundancy; selecting the best sources available; and, finding specific, desired information. The Internet represents a major attack of information indigestion—we are all overwhelmed by it, like having eaten Thanksgiving dinner, Christmas dinner, and a New Year's Eve banquet all at once. Information management vis-à-vis the Internet is a whole new skill and is becoming a whole new profession.

First, suggest that your students use the strategies in Chapter 7 to find keypals in Canada. These direct connections with real Canadians will be one excellent way to test firsthand the archival information that your students will discover on databases. Because most Canadians speak English, an e-mail connection with Canadians is easy and should be great fun.

Then, start the Web-walking part of the task. You may want to divide your class into several groups, each group working on a different section of the alphabet book. You may also want the groups to be responsible for a segment of the alphabet, such as A–E, F–J, K–O, P–T, U–Z. (or because A–E is inherently easier than U–Z, you might want to mix the letters up: Group 1: A, F, K, P, U; Group 2: B, G, L, Q, V; Group 3: C, H, M, R, W; Group 4: D, I, N,

S, Z; and Group 5: E, J, O, T, Y, Z.) When the Internet work has been completed, your students need to lay out the book and make it ready for publication. After it is published, partner your class with a class at a lower-grade level so that your students may share their information about Canada with the younger kids. Before the cross-grade collaboration, give your students some guidance on what to expect from the younger kids: how to relate to them; how to share the book with them; and, how to let them enjoy the book. This may be your students' first lesson in teaching; the teacher's job is not to show off but to facilitate the learning of the student. The learner's joy in finding out and knowing is greater when they've done it mostly on their own.

Evaluation

By compiling the several groups' work, your class can produce a full ABC Book of Canada for sharing with another class. The process of bringing the various parts and pieces together can become a beneficial formative assessment. Each group can evaluate their own and others' work individually and in relation to the whole. Decisions will have to be made about what to include and exclude; what the balance, style, focus, look, and feel will be like; and, the specifics of typography and book production. You can make this book as simple or complex as you and your students like. It can take whatever physical form you choose—certainly an online computer document, but also a printed-out hard-copy edition with pictures, graphs, charts, prose, facts, maps, stories, and whatever else your students want to include. One major proof of the pudding will be in how well your class project goes over with the students' younger partners; the kids in the class down the hall. The standard of assessment and evaluation during this phase needs to be the younger kids' reception and enjoyment of your "Online ABC Book of Canada." After the cross-grade presentation, engage your students in a discussion of how it went with the other class. Remind your students of the points you will have made in preparing them to work with the younger class (see "Procedures" above), and use those suggestions as a check list against which to evaluate the collaborative experience. This evaluation will be a self-assessment conducted by your students of their own work for the younger students.

Visit Canada via the Internet

⬤ Yahoo: Canada

http://www.yahoo.ca/

Yahoo has it's own Web site on Canada. From this directory you can find information on each province and territory. This is probably the first site to visit to get an idea of the scope of information that is available.

⬤ The Flags and Arms of Canada

http://www.cs.cmu.edu/afs/cs.cmu.edu/user/
clamen/misc/Canadiana/CA-Flags.html

Get a look at the flags and coat of arms for each province and territory.

⬤ About Canada

http://canada.gc.ca/canadiana/cdaind_e.html

Learn many facts about Canada in either French or English. This governmental site is part of the Primary Internet Site of Canada at **http://canada.gc.ca/main_e.html**.

⬤ Symbols of Canada

http://canada.gc.ca/canadiana/symb_e.html

The Web site to learn about the meaning of the emblems and symbols of Canada.

⬤ Federal Links

http://canada.gc.ca/depts/major/depind_e.html

An alphabetical listing of links to every department in the Canadian government.

CIA Fact Book of Canada

http://www.odci.gov/cia/publications/factbook/ca.html

A text-only page that tells you about the geography, economy, people, and everything else about Canada. You can view a map of Canada here at **http://www.odci.gov/cia/publications/nsolo/factbook/map-gif/ca-150.gif**.

Canadiana: The Canada Resource Page

http://www.cs.cmu.edu/afs/cs.cmu.edu/user/clamen/misc/Canadiana/README.html

A general information page with links to news and information, facts and figures, travel and tourism, government, politics and history, science and education, technology, heritage, culture and entertainment, and finally general links. This is a huge Web site.

Defacto: Geographical Facts About Canada

http://www-nais.ccm.emr.ca/defacto/

This Web site reads like a trivia game. Where is the longest river in Canada? How many lakes are there in Saskatchewan? Each paragraph is written in English and French.

Tour of Canada Without Leaving Your Desk

http://www.cs.cmu.edu/afs/cs.cmu.edu/user/clamen/misc/Canadiana/Travelogue.html

All the links you need to see, hear and read about Canada. This Web site is a good source for alphabetical information. It is written in both French and English.

◑ Canadian Government Information on the Internet

http://dsp-psd.pwgsc.gc.ca/dsp-psd/Reference/cgii_index-e.html

Leads you to information about the peoples, provinces, and territories of Canada.

◑ The National Post Online

http://www.nationalpost.com/

It's always wise to know the news, so click here to see it from the Canadian perspective.

◑ Natural Resources Canada

http://www.nrcan.gc.ca/ (home page)
http://www.nrcan.gc.ca/homepage/toc_e.shtml (English page)

Click on any of the icons and be transported to one of the various departments that deal with Canadian natural resources.

◑ Weather from Environment Canada

http://www.doe.ca/weather_e.html

Here you can get weather forecasts for every area of Canada, as well as maps, charts, and satellite imagery. In Canada, temperatures are shown in degrees Celsius, not Fahrenheit. This would make a good exercise for converting one temperature system to the other.

To start your students thinking about Canada in terms of the ABC's, I have provided a sample ABeCeDarium and quiz. Each letter features a question, and they can Web-walk the Canadian sites mentioned above to find the answers, filling out the URLs as proof of their discoveries. After they have practiced using this page, it's their turn to make up their own twenty-six letter ABeCeDarium.

An ABC book of anything provides a fun way to learn, no matter what topic you choose. It is a natural way for your students (no matter what grade level) to write and draw their knowledge and share that knowledge with someone else. The ABC approach allows your students' minds to rove widely and gather the fragments of information needed to give factual substance to "in-depth" discussions. As you and your students visit Canada on the Internet, discussion opportunities will arise. This is your chance to develop higher-order thinking skills that have been based on the information found in an ABC book. If your students are like many I have worked with, they will soon be producing ABC books on all sorts of topics. Just this past year, I've had students work on ABC books of Paris, Fish, Weather, the Rainforest, as well as various states in the US. Everyone seems to like this activity.

A Sample Internet ABeCeDarium of Canada

A is for Aleut-http://
How many Native Canadian peoples can you name?

B is for Banff-http://
Where is Lake Louise?

C is for Calgary Stampede-http://
Who does the stampeding?

D is for Dogwood (provincial flower of British Columbia)-http://
Where is British Columbia?

E is for Elizabeth the Queen-http://
Is the Queen of England still the Queen of Canada?

F is for French language—http://
How many people speak French in Canada?
How many people speak Ukranian and other non-English languages?

G is for Gaspar Bay, Nova Scotia—http://
How cold does it get in the northern parts of Canada?

H is for Hudson's Bay—http://
What was the Hudson's Bay Company, and for whom was it named?

I is for Inuit—http://
Now how many native Canadian peoples can you name?

J is for Jasper National Park—http://
Do Canadians or Americans do a better job of taking care of nature?

K is for Kingston, Ontario—http://
Who named Kingston and why?

L is for Loonie—http://
What's a loon?

M is for Maple Leaf Flag—http://
What else in Canada is called "the Leafs?"

N is for Niagara Falls—http://
Half of Niagara Falls is in Canada; where is the other half?

O is for Ottawa—http://
Can you name all of the provinces and their capital cities?

P is for Parliament and the Prime Minister—http://
How does Canadian government differ from American government?

Q is for Quebec City—http://
Quebec City is the only walled city in North America and the capital of New France. What else is called "Quebec?"

R is for Regina, Saskatchewan—http://
Who was the Regina they had in mind when they named the town?

S is for Saint Lawrence Seaway—http://
From where and to where and between where does it run?

T is for Toonie—http://
This new coin rhymes with Loonie. What does it stand for?

U is for Union Corner Provincial Park, P.E.I.—http://
What are the Maritimes?

V is for Victoria Island, B.C.—http://
Where does America stop and Canada start? What is the Pig War?

W is for Winnipeg, Manitoba—http://
The name "Winnipeg" derives from what language?

X is for xenophobia—http://
What is the basic Canadian attitude toward foreigners?

Y is for Yukon Territory—http://
Gold fever! What can you find out about the American gold rush into Canada?

Z is for Zones—http://
How many time zones does Canada have, and how do Canadians write the zip codes that indicate their postal zones?

ABC Web Site Reference Chart

Names: _____   Date: _____

Today we viewed the following Web sites for the ABC book:

http:// _____   Title: _____

http:// _____   Title: _____

http:// _____   Title: _____

http:// _____   Title: _____

http:// _____   Title: _____

We plan to use the following Web site for information on the letter _____ :

http:// _____   Title: _____

We plan to write the following information on that letter:

_____

_____

_____

We plan to use the following Web site for information on the letter _____ :

http:// _____   Title: _____

We plan to write the following information on that letter:

_____

_____

_____

This information should be completed for each letter used by each group.

Evaluation Rubric for "The ABCs of Canada"

Assessment Area	Exemplary	Proficient	Not Yet
Content and ideas of the book (or Web site)	• Ideas are clearly presented • Content follows ABC order • Each listing has an excellent explanation • Each listing has a URL reference	• Ideas are somewhat clear • Content follows ABC order • 1–3 alphabet listings are missing • Each listing has a good explanation • Some URL references missing or incomplete	• Ideas present are unclear • Content not in order • Many letters are missing • Listings are unclear • Most references are incomplete
Layout of the book	• Excellent use of graphics • Excellent use of white space on page to make reading of the book easy	• Good use of graphics • Good use of white space so the reader wants to read the book	• Little or no use of graphics • Pages are cramped making it difficult to read the book
Sharing the book with another class	• Excellent rapport with other students • Very patient when working with younger students; answered all questions and concerns with ease	• Good rapport with younger students • Patient when working with younger students	• Reluctant to share with younger students • Impatient when working with younger students
Internet Experience	• Used many different Web sites to find the best information • Contacted Canadians on e-mail to get firsthand information • Used excellent search strategies • ABC Web site reference charts are up to date • Relied on three to four Web sites to find information	• Relied on three to four Web sites to find information • Wrote e-mail to one Canadian to obtain first-hand information • Used good search strategies to find information • ABC Web site reference charts are used regularly	• Obtained information from one Web site • Did not utilize e-mail to contact a Canadian • Search strategies were not used effectively • ABC Web site reference charts were kept irregularly
Mechanics	• Excellent grammar, punctuation and spelling • ABC book is easy to read and follow	• Good grammar, punctuation and spelling • Errors do not "get in the way" of the story line	• Faulty grammar, punctuation and spelling • ABC book is difficult to read because of errors
Cooperation	• Students worked well together • Students shared the work load fairly • Students solved problems in a fair manner	• Students worked together with little strife • Burden of work done by small part of the group • Students solved most problems in a fair manner	• Students did not work well together • Burden of work done by one member of the group • Teacher intervention was needed to solve problems

Chapter 11

Virtually Together in D.C.

I n all elementary, middle, and high schools, students in the U.S. study American government. Many schools sponsor trips to Washington, D.C. every year for selected fifth-, eighth-, and eleventh-graders. Before your students take their actual trip to Washington, D.C., however, I suggest that they (and you!) go on a virtual tour of the city. If your school does not provide for such a trip, that's an even better reason to take this cybertour.

The Internet sources that make a virtual trip possible will also make Washington more interesting and meaningful when your students actually arrive there. The following Internet-based tour guide to D.C., will prepare your students for the real geography, history and grandeur that they will encounter in our capital city.

✎ In Your Classroom

A Virtual Tour of Washington, D.C.

The first time my mother visited Washington, D.C., she made a startling discovery: The White House and the Capitol were two different buildings in two different locations. She was surprised! Somehow, despite news broadcasts about what the President had said at "the White House" as opposed to what Congress had done "on the Hill," the two had coalesced in her mind.

With this lesson, you can familiarize your students with the map of Washington, D.C., as well as with the significance of many of the buildings, monuments, and other landmarks that make Washington the living, open history book of America.

Goals

- To give students a better understanding of the geographical layout and historical relevance composition of our nation's capital by taking a virtual tour.

- To help them understand our democratic system of government better by experiencing the real-estate of government.

- To get them ready and eager to go to Washington.

Rationale

Washington, D.C., is the seat of the American national government. When students know the significance of the various official edifices, they tend to develop a better understanding of our country, our history, our leaders (past and present), and our representative democracy. When students have an idea about the nature of the U.S. Government, the location of the seat of power, and can put a face to famous people and recognize important buildings, they gain a better understanding of what it means to be an American.

Objectives

- Using map skills, students will locate the nation's capital, points of historical interest in the city and determine the best routes to travel in the City.

- Students will be able to explain what takes place at each site, and the meaning for America of the following public edifices: the White House, the Supreme Court, the Capitol Building, the Smithsonian Institution, the Treasury, the Library of Congress, the Lincoln Memorial, the Washington Monument, the Jefferson Memorial, the Vietnam Memorial, etc.

- Students will determine ten places they want to visit in Washington, D.C., explain in writing why they want to visit them, create a personal tour-map of Washington, D.C. describing the tour that they want to take, and create a bookmark tour that they will show to the class.

Procedures

Set the stage by telling your class that they are going on a trip (either a real, or virtual or both) to Washington, D.C. While they are thinking about the trip they are going to take, hold a brainstorming session to determine what your students already know about Washington, D.C. Prepare a semantic map or web that has Washington, D.C. in the center, then create branches for each piece of information your students give you about the City. Show your students photographs, post cards, and/or videos of Washington, D.C. Share with your students books, travel guides, articles and Web sites on Washington, D.C. After this, they should be ready for their virtual tour, which will prepare them for an actual tour they might take.

Using the bookmarks at the end of this lesson, challenge your students to locate ten people, places or things they want to visit. Then they can prepare a group set of Washington, D.C. bookmarks which will allow the class to take a virtual tour of the special sites in our nation's capital. I highly recommend that you set your home page to The White House at **http://www.whitehouse.gov** as there is a very pornographic page at whitehouse.com. Students might accidentally get to the .com page and become very embarrassed. To stop this from happening, set the home page at whitehouse.gov and that way there are no surprises. As usual for these exercises, your students should work in small groups and the groups need to decide how to work in harmony. Each day your student groups are online, they should complete a site log relating the Web sites they visited during that Internet session, the Web sites they selected for their bookmark list, and the reasons why they selected those sites. Resourceful students may be able to tell you about the National Arboretum, the National Gallery, the exhibits at the Library of Congress, or they will find other sites of special interest to themselves. At the end of the desired time, your groups of students will have chosen the ten places they want to visit, written a paper explaining why they want to visit those places, and will have prepared a set of bookmarks for a virtual tour that other members of the class can take. As a culminating activity to share the bookmarked virtual tours, have each group of students select three to five "favorite places" they want to visit in Washington, D.C. Have them present their virtual tour for their classmates, showing and explaining the places they want to visit, and telling why those places are significant to them and to the country. If each group in your class selects three different sites, they will have organized a thorough virtual tour of the city to prepare them for the actual tour-to-come.

If you are going on an actual trip to Washington, D.C., you might want to include a section on the economics of lodging, meals and transportation. This adds another facet to the lesson, one that is most important: budgeting time and money.

You and your students will find many more Internet sites on Washington than I have provided. To go along with what you can discover via the Internet, use other electronic library resources, such as Encarta, a CD-ROM program with a lot of great information about Washington, D.C.

For a thought-provoking, optional capstone project, propose that each student design his or her own D.C. monument, draw a sketch of it, and be ready to explain the following to the class: what it would look like; where it would be located in D.C.; and what it means or represents.

Evaluation

By the end of the virtual tour of Washington, D.C., your students will be familiar with several of the important buildings and monuments in the city. Your students should be able to tell you the significance of the various monuments. The evaluation rubric for this lesson (at the end of the chapter) has the following parts: Web site Logs; Ideas, Content and Organization of Virtual Trip Bookmarks; Ideas, Content and Organization of Written Report; Mechanics; and, Cooperation.

Starting Points for a Washington, D.C. Virtual Tour

⬤ The White House

http://www.whitehouse.gov

A trip to Washington, D.C. means a visit to the White House. At the virtual White House are links for the President and Vice President, an Interactive Citizens' Handbook, White House History and Tours, Past Presidents and First Families, Art in the President's House and Tours, The Virtual Library, The Briefing

Room, and the White House for Kids. I particularly like the links for Kids and Past Presidents. I highly recommend that you designate this as the home page for the lesson and program your Web browser so kids can always get back here.

⬤ The White House Collection of American Crafts

http://nmaa-ryder.si.edu/collections/exhibits/whc/index.html

American crafts made from ceramic, wood, fiber, metal and glass are displayed at this Web site.

⬤ Yahoo, Washington, D.C.

http://dc.yahoo.com/

Organized the same way as the Yahoo directory, but all the topics relate to Washington, D.C.

⬤ National Capital Parks

http://www.nps.gov/nacc/

The place to go for links to the Washington Monument, Lincoln Memorial, Jefferson Memorial, Vietnam Veteran's Memorial, among other important National Park sites in Washington, D.C.

 The National Park Service

⬤ City Net: Washington, D.C.

http://www.city.net/countries/united_states/district_of_columbia/washington

Another resource directory that is easy to use.

◉ Clickable Map of Washington, D.C.

http://sc94.ameslab.gov:80/TOUR/tour.html

A small (37K) and accurate map of the Federal Area to give you a
general idea of the location of everything you are going to visit.

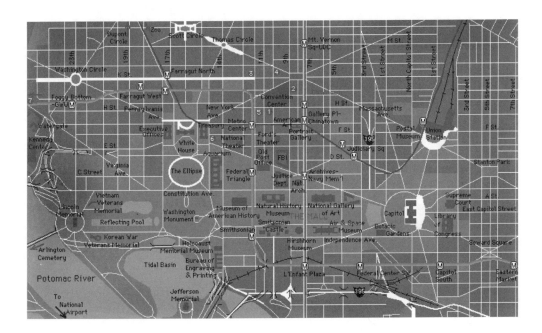

◉ Travel on the Metro System in D.C.

http://www.washingtonpost.com/wp-srv/local/longterm/
metro/ (from the Washington Post) and
http://www.wmata.com/USINGMET/systemmap.htm (from
the Metrorail system)

Make a copy of this map and use it for your actual tour of Washington, D.C. (I've lived in D.C. and this map is a BIG help!) Click
on any of the stations and see information about that individual
station. A great resource for the traveler.

- **The Declaration of Independence**
  http://lcweb2.loc.gov/const/declar.html

- **The U.S. Constitution**
  http://lcweb2.loc.gov/const/const.html

Some Monuments and Memorials

- **The FDR Memorial**
  http://www.nps.gov/fdrm/index2.htm

- **The Jefferson Memorial**
  http://www.nps.gov/thje/index2.htm

- **The Lincoln Memorial**
  http://www.nps.gov/linc/index2.htm
  http://sc94.ameslab.gov/TOUR/linmem.html

- **Mount Vernon**
  http://www.mountvernon.org/

- **The Vietnam Memorial**
  http://www.nps.gov/vive/index2.htm
  http://www.vietvet.org/thewall.htm
  http://thewall-usa.com/index.html

- **The Washington Monument**
  http://sc94.ameslab.gov/TOUR/washmon.html
  http://www.nps.gov/wamo/monument/monument.htm

- **The Old Executive Office Building**
  http://www.whitehouse.gov/WH/Tours/OEOB/html/
  Welcome.html

The Congress

The best source for everything about the Senate and House of Representatives, is the Congressional Record, which features important speeches from the last two congresses, as well as information on how the legislative branch of government works.

- **The House of Representatives**
  http://www.house.gov/

- **The Senate**
  http://www.senate.gov/

- **Thomas (named for Thomas Jefferson)**
  http://thomas.loc.gov

- **Congress.Org**
  http://207.168.215.81/

Cabinet Level and Other Agencies

To find out information about the President's Cabinet, click on some of these links.

- **The President's Cabinet**
  http://www.whitehouse.gov/WH/Cabinet/html/
  cabinet_links-plain.html

- **A current list of cabinet secretaries**
  http://www.whitehouse.gov/WH/
  Cabinet/html/secretary.html

- **The Treasury Department**
  http://www.ustreas.gov/

- **The Department of Justice**
  http://www.usdoj.gov/

- **The Department of Defense**
  http://www.defenselink.mil/

- **The Department of Education**
  http://www.ed.gov/

THE
U.S. Department of
EDUCATION

Other Departments of Government

- **The Federal Web Locator**
  http://www.law.vill.edu/Fed-Agency/

- **FedWorld**
  http://www.fedworld.gov/

- **The Federal Bureau of Investigation**
  http://www.fbi.gov/

- **The Central Intelligence Agency**
  http://www.odci.gov/cia/

Welcome to the **Central Intelligence Agency**

Libraries and Museums

The cultural life of Washington is a rich one: museums, scientific institutions, art galleries, libraries, and more. D.C. is a showplace to the world of the best that America has to offer.

● Library of Congress

http://www.loc.gov/

View three excellent presentations: "The American Memory" which looks at American history at **http://lcweb2.loc.gov/ ammem/**; "Thomas" (mentioned above in Congress); and "Exhibitions" at **http://lcweb.loc.gov/exhibits/**.

● The Smithsonian Institution

http://www.si.edu/

Follow the links to find out information about each of the various museums that make up the Smithsonian Institution. This can be a confusing Web site.

● The Natural History Museum

http://www.mnh.si.edu/nmnhweb.html

See the Hope Diamond at **http:// naturalpartners.org/VirtualTour/ Tour/Second/Hope/index.html**. See the Insect Zoo at **http:// nmnhwww.si.edu/VirtualTour/Tour/ Second/InsectZoo/index.html**. The Hall of Bones lets kids observe the relationship among animals at **http:/ /nmnhwww.si.edu/VirtualTour/Tour/ Second/Bones/index.html**.

©Copyright Smithsonian

● Air and Space Museum

http://www.nasm.si.edu/

● National Zoo

http://www.si.edu/natzoo/

Other Interesting Links to Washington, D.C.

● **The National Holocaust Museum**
http://www.ushmm.org/index.html

● **The National Cathedral**
http://www.cathedral.org/cathedral/

Other Tours

You have an idea now how to design virtual tours for other cities. Using this model, I've seen tours made for towns and cities in the U.S. and for schools. A virtual tour of your hometown is a challenging class project and would look great on your class home page (see Chapter 4). If you decide to make one up, please send it to me at **cotton@instruction.com** and I'll post the address on the Web site for The Online Classroom at **http://www.csuchico.edu/online_classroom**.

Washington, D.C. Web Site Log

Group Name: _____   Date: _____

Members: _____   _____

_____   _____

Today we viewed the following Web sites:

http:// _____   Title: _____

http:// _____   Title: _____

http:// _____   Title: _____

http:// _____   Title: _____

The most important Web site we viewed was http:// _____

It was important to our virtual tour of Washington, D.C. because:

_____

_____

Another important Web site was http:// _____

It was important to our virtual tour of Washington, D.C. because:

_____

_____

Today we learned the following about Washington, D.C.:

_____

_____

Describe the Web sites you want to include in your virtual tour and why you want to include them. You may use the back of the paper if you run out of room.

_____

_____

Evaluation Rubric for "Virtually Together in D.C."

Assessment Area	Exemplary	Proficient	Not Yet
Web Site Logs	• Completed for each day online • Responses to items show original thought processes • Reflect excellent use of Internet time	• Most days online are logged in • Responses to logs are satisfactory • Reflect good use of Internet time	• Web site logs are incomplete • Reflect poor use of Internet time
Ideas, Content and Organization of Virtual Trip	• Bookmarks are in order • Bookmarks show variety of themes • Ideas are clearly presented • Interesting sites are chosen that hold attention of audience	• Bookmarks are not in correct order • Bookmarks show only one or two themes • Ideas are somewhat clear • Most sites are interesting to the audience	• Bookmarks are not organized • Bookmarks show no theme • Ideas present are unclear • Boring and does not hold the attention of the audience
Ideas, Content and Organization of Written Report	• Report and bookmarks work together well • Report is well organized • Content of report relates to Washington, D.C. tour • Excellent explanation of significance of each chosen Web site	• Report and bookmarks coincide • Report shows good organization • Content mostly relates to Washington, D.C. tour • Good explanation of significance of each chosen Web site	• Report and bookmarks do not coincide • Report disorganized • Content wanders • Poor explanation or no explanation of significance for Web sites chosen
Mechanics	• Excellent grammar, punctuation and spelling • Easy to read aloud	• Good grammar, punctuation and spelling • Most parts easy to read	• Faulty grammar, punctuation and spelling • Awkward to read out loud
Cooperation	• Students worked well together • Students shared the work load fairly • Students solved problems in a fair manner	• Students worked together with little strife • Burden of work done by small part of the group • Students solved most problems in a fair manner	• Students did not work well together • Burden of work done by one member of the group • Teacher intervention was needed to solve problems

Chapter 12:
Get a Job!

One of the benefits of an education is that it can help you get a job. The first step towards getting a job is writing a résumé. The Internet is a great resource for finding out more than you want to know about conceiving and writing and targeting a résumé, finding a job, interviewing for it, and selling yourself personally and professionally. The purpose of this chapter is to give senior high-school students the chance to explore the various résumé Web pages and craft their own résumés in preparation for a job interview. This résumé can be either for a job right now or part of an application for college. Either way, résumé writing is a skill that every student will need upon graduation and for the rest of their working lives.

✎ In Your Classroom

Job Hunting with a Safety Net

Goal

Understand and craft an effective résumé.

Rationale

Writing a powerful résumé is an important skill that you use throughout your working life. Every professional needs to keep his or her résumé up-to-date because in today's world of unstable employment, one never knows when it will be needed. Practice in résumé writing will help high-school students learn what it takes to produce a résumé that leads to a job.

Objectives

- Students will read Web pages about résumés.

- Students will construct a résumé.

- Students will use the résumé in a job-interview simulation.

Procedures

Set the stage by showing your students a variety of résumés. Some of the résumés should be very good and some should be just the opposite. Discuss the aspects of each type of résumé. There are résumés and résumé guides on the Web, so samples are easy to find.

Also discuss writing a Web site Summary Log. This is a notebook page that lists the Web sites the student viewed, including the URL and Title of the Web site and a brief summary of what was found there. The Web site Summary Log can be referred to often, as it is sometimes not possible or advisable for students to bookmark Web sites on a classroom computer. The Web site Summary Log can be considered an offline bookmark.

How to find résumés on the Web

The first step is to use a Web search engine, like WebCrawler or InfoSeek, to search for words like "résumé," "résumé writing," "curriculum vitae," or "vita," and see what you get. Tell your students that they are to develop résumés that will help them get jobs or assist them with their college applications. Show them various sites on the Internet that help with résumé development, and let them glean the information offered there. For students who have not had a job, have them list volunteer work they have done, school and/or church organizations they have belonged to, or babysitting for younger siblings or neighbors. The final product is each student's design of an honest, workable, effective résumé that can be used to find a job or as part of a college entrance application or application for a scholarship, loan, or grant. Have some parents or community members who have experience in the business world or in higher-education admissions be part of a mock résumé panel. Ask them to look at working drafts of the résumés and make comments and offer suggestions.

Once students have composed their résumés based on examples and advice chosen from various Web sites (and résumé volunteers), they need to prepare their texts on a computer using a word-processing or desktop publishing program. Proper software will allow them to design a résumé that is attractive and useful. A résumé that is maintained on a computer file can be easily updated—which is a never-ending task. When your students get another job, finish another class, or accomplish something else they are proud of, they will want to add the accomplishments to their résumés.

The pros in the field say that a résumé should be tailored to fit the job. A generic "one size fits all" résumé is often an ineffective strategy. With a computerized version of your résumé, you can tailor it to meet the specifics of a job description. A résumé is a personal advertisement.

Before printing a final copy of a résumé, have your students set it aside for a day or two, then reread it and check to see that it says what they want it to say. Have several friends and colleagues proofread it to see if it conveys the intended message: Hire me! I'm the right person for the job! Résumé writing is, therefore, a high-interest opportunity for group collaboration as your students read and critique each other's résumés.

You can also find résumés (on- and offline) that have been hastily crafted. Call attention to these blemishes in other people's self-ads, and engage in a discussion on how to put one's best foot forward in a global, public display of one's life, accomplishments, and talents. A résumé does not have to be boring or dull, but it does need to be professional looking and positive sounding.

For a culminating activity, invite back your "résumé helpers" or a couple of parents or local business people to stage mock interviews with your students based on their résumés.

Variations on a Theme

If you have students who have little or no work experience, they can develop a résumé for a historical figure, a character in a novel, or for a member of their family. Students can also use this lesson as a way to learn how to set goals. They can write a two-part résumé: Part I is an explanation of what they have accomplished to date; Part II shows what they want to accomplish in five years (or after they graduate from college).

Evaluation

The final product is the proof of the lesson. Are the résumés honest, realistic, workable documents? Will they be effective in the eyes of a prospective employer or admissions officer? Are they attractive as well as useful?

Listed below are some Web sites where you and your students will find useful information about résumé writing. A few sources are specifically for high-school students, while some sources are specifically for college students and professionals. By looking at this mixture, your students will discover how important this skill is in gaining future employment. These are links your students can use when developing ideas for their own résumés.

Internet Help with Résumé Writing

The Résumé Tutor from the University of Minnesota

http://www1.umn.edu/ohr/ecep/resume/

Excellent Web site that leads you through the questions you have to ask when creating a résumé. The easy to use six-step tutor tells you about résumé format (job objective, experience, activities/interests), writing style, how to be critical about your résumé, and lets you see some sample résumés. It's a great page to learn about creating a positive advertisement for *you*.

⬤ How to Write a Résumé (Trinity College)

http://www.trincoll.edu/admin/career/how_to_guides/resume.shtml

While aimed at the soon-to-be college graduate, this page has some great hints on how to make a résumé exciting. Look for the list of action verbs. It's a good one.

⬤ Rebecca Smith's eRésumés and Resources

http://www.eresumes.com/

A very comprehensive look at how to write a résumé for the 21st century. You can view résumés online as well as learn more about style, format and content.

⬤ Important Career Information

http://www.espan.com/docs/index.html#resume

A master list of links about how to find and keep a job. Included are links to résumé writing and interviewing.

⬤ Top Ten Technical Résumé-Writing Tips

http://www.taos.com/resumetips.html

While this might not be an interesting page to look at, the ten writing tips are good ones and they reinforce everything that the other Web sites mention. Scroll down the page and find answers to common questions about layout, use of pictures, and the like.

⬤ A Guide to Effective Résumé Writing

http://www.ceweekly.wa.com/helpful/grw.html

This site provides guidance on how to write, lay out, and deliver a résumé. Look at a sample résumé at **http://www.ceweekly.wa.com/helpful/sampres.html**.

⬤ Career Builder's How to Guide to Résumés

http://www.careerbuilder.com/gh_res_htg.html

A simple-to-use guide introducing your students to résumés, how to format and write them, followed by additional résumé resources and lastly, how to create an electronic résumé.

⬤ The Wall Street Journal: Careers

http://careers.wsj.com/?content=cwc-resumes.htm

This page is written for the professional seeking another position, however it has some great pointers on how to write a résumé and cover letter. It might be too advanced for some students, but teachers may choose to use it as a resource.

● The Campus Market: Résumé Building

http://www.campusaccess.com/4.html

This Web page from Canada has a university focus. If you want to write a résumé as part of your college application, this is the page for you. There are tips on interviewing, networking and how to survive college, in addition to how to write an effective résumé. While the page does not have lots of graphics, the text is informative and easy to read.

If you are writing a résumé for entrance into a college, there are a number of Web sites that will help you find the way. To map out your future, go to **http://www.mapping-your-future.org./** and find out about selecting a college, and finding a career. If you need to know about financial aid and scholarships, go to FastWeb at **http://fastweb.com**. Another good source is Scholarships on the Web at **http://collegescholarships.com/**. These Web sites will give you some information about college. If you are searching for a career, you might want to take a personality test. There are several on the Web, but the Keirsey Temperament Sorter II is easy to take and gives instant results. To find it, go to **http:// www.keirsey.com/cgi-bin/keirsey/newkts.cgi** and take the seventy-item forced-choice test. When you are finished the answers are analyzed and a personality "type" is indicated. Please be advised that the results of these tests are not always accurate.

It's easier for beginners to visualize their own résumés after they have seen some samples. Not many teenagers are seeking jobs over the Internet, so there are few résumés by high-school students posted on the Internet. Thousands of résumés written by high-school and college graduates, however, are posted. These offer excellent examples of form and substance, both good and bad. To find a comprehensive up-to-date list, go to Yahoo and type in "résumé," scroll down the huge list until you see "individual résumé" and start clicking away. You will see there are many different examples of résumés on the Internet.

A Final Word

A résumé is a necessity for getting almost any job: be it truck driver, machinist, grocery worker, teacher, computer programmer or somewhere in management. When your students have access to the myriad of résumés on the Internet for guidance, they can develop the skills needed to write a résumé. When your students have been introduced to the skill of résumé writing, they will be better prepared for their future.

Evaluation Rubric for "Get a Job!"

Assessment Area	Exemplary	Proficient	Not Yet
Organization	• Job objective indicated • Each section of the résumé is clearly denoted • Logical scheme (either chronological or from most to least important)	• Job objective indicated • Each section of the résumé is somewhat easy to find • Somewhat logical scheme	• No job objective indicated • There is no coherent organization evident
Content	• Each section is consistent with other sections • All content is honest and realistic	• Each section is readable • Content is valid	• Content questionable
Style	• Many active verbs are used • Excellent writing style	• Some active verbs are used • Good writing style	• Few or no active verbs • Style is lacking
Mechanics	• Excellent grammar, punctuation and spelling • Proofread by other students and edited	• Good grammar, punctuation and spelling • Evidence of some proofreading by another student • Evidence of editing	• Faulty grammar, punctuation and spelling • No evidence of proofreading
Internet Experience	• Used Internet time well • Searched for other online resources • Maintained a daily summary log of Web sites visited	• Followed the sources given in the chapter • Maintained a summary log of Web sites visited 3 to 4 times a week	• Did not follow resources given • Did not search out new resources • Did not maintain summary Web site log

Chapter 13:
A Book an Hour

T eaching strategies take on a whole new life when adapted for use with the Internet. With this chapter, you and your students can practice using your Web browser while reading a book in an hour. "A Book an Hour" is an excellent and speedy way to introduce a whole book to middle- and high-school students, whether a novel, history or science text, or literary classic.

Prior to high-tech, the strategy has been:

- Divide a book into chapters or sections so that small groups of students can read the parts and collaborate in preparing summaries.

- A spokesperson for each group, beginning with the group that has read the first segment of the book, tells that group's summary. The next segment's group does the same, and so on until the whole story had been told to the class.

- As the summaries are read, develop a master chart either on the board or an overhead transparency to map out the story according to the summaries.

- At the end, the whole class works on a summary of the summaries of the several parts.

Together, your class will have read, reported, and summarized a whole literary classic in a single period, if the book is not too long. When I've used this approach, I've found that I needed a minimum of two class periods for the strategy to work best, and I also needed more time when I used the strategy with a class for the first time. In addition, the book needs to described to the class beforehand so they have an idea of what is going to happen. Although this approach does not allow for a close reading of the text, it is a quick and easy way to introduce a work of literature to your students. They might get the idea that "literature" can be fun to read. This *hors d'oeuvres* approach will whet their appetites for more reading on their own.

In Your Classroom

An Online Book an Hour

An electronic version of "a book an hour" might go something like this: Instead of dividing up hard copy into chapters or sections, your students search out, download and divvy up, then read an electronic copy of their respective parts. If the book is not too long and is accessible online, students could read their sections directly from the Internet, but I don't recommend that. There is no point in tying up the connection that long. More logical and less expensive, I suggest downloading the book onto a hard drive or diskette, converting it to the class word-processing package, dividing the text into segments with block-and-copy moves, then have your students read their segments either on their computers or print out a hard copy of the text. Every student gets to read his or her own copy; and, at the end, a saved backup copy of the whole book becomes the readable property of every student, the first volume in their electronic library.

While your students are reading their sections of the book on their computer screens, they can also be taking notes; multitasking between two files. One file is the copy for the book, the other is a word-processing file for notes. They can also write notes using pen and paper. Whatever method is used, your students can record their thoughts instantly and easily, and build their summaries as they read. Printed paper books, even with the widest of margins, do not allow for this extent of editorializing as one reads.

Using the block-copy-move function and the split-screen, your students can assemble their electronic notes into a draft of a summary, then rewrite and reformat it with word processing-based ease. Each member of the group can read the draft-summaries of all the other members, typing out comments in shared-journal fashion. Then, when they meet in their groups to talk over the details and polish a final summary of that group's segment, they will have the benefit of already having read one another's individual comments and summaries.

Goal

Your students will become familiar with a classic work of literature by reading, commenting, summarizing, and crafting a summary of summaries of the selection, in one or two class periods.

Rationale

It is sometimes difficult to generate interest in "the dead poets" and other classical authors. Their literary legacy is, nevertheless, a major part of the culture of our society and the light of our aesthetic life. However, an electronic "skimming" of one of their works can involve students who normally would be put off from the story by old-fashioned language and a slower-than-usual pace. When your students become familiar with these fine and enjoyable works of literary art in a meaningful yet "painless" way—and at the warp-speed of a video game—then fewer of them will register the universal complaint: "This is boring!" When they have a sense of the overall plot and characters now in mind, they will be encouraged to read the full version of the classic on their own.

Objectives

- Students will download, read, comment upon and summarize a segment of a piece of literature.

- Students will discuss segment summaries and create a summary of summaries for the whole book.

- Students will collaborate on reading a classic work of literature in a short amount of time to whet their appetite for other pieces of literature.

- After several books have been read using these electronic strategies, students can compare and discuss the various works of classic literature in relation to each other.

Optional Objective

Publish a Class "Illustrated Classic Comic"

- Students draw (either freehand or using a computer drawing program) pictures for each summary. Make a notebook of the pictures, each picture to be accompanied by its respective summary, with the "grand summation" at the end to complete the project.

Procedures

To generate enthusiasm, you need to stage the first event well. If you hook up with a smooth Internet connection and high-interest electronic books the first time you use the strategy, then you will be off to a good start. If you are studying the Romantic Period, for example, you will definitely want your students to read the works of Edgar Allan Poe. Show your class that you have only a few copies of the book, but through the Internet, everyone is going to read chapters of this book and make their own comments about the significance of the story. At this point, the class Web-walks to Poe (you will already have located the site because you want this lesson to go rapidly), and your students take it from there. To see online versions of many of the works by Edgar Allan Poe, check out "The Incomplete Works of EAP" at **http://www.comnet.ca/ ~forrest/works.html**. To save some time, the alphabetical bibliography of Poe's work is located at **http://bau2.uibk.ac.at/sg/poe/ Alpha.html**.

Select the Poe title you want. Have your students block and copy the text, divide it into segments, and copy it onto diskettes for reading and annotating. Have your students work in small groups. If you have more students than you have computers, then each group of three or four students can cluster around a computer. Let one student act as electronic scribe, seated at the keyboard, while the others read the screen and offer comments.

As a regular routine in an English or Language Arts class, this strategy can be used about once every other week quite effectively. Students enjoy it and look forward to doing it again and again. You may assign your students to do the surfing to find next week's book.

Evaluation

The various possible versions of this activity are easy to evaluate: Did the chapter/segment summary-writing work? Did your students take hold of their parts of the book and understand them? Did the summary of summaries work—is it logical and accurate? Is there a notebook of summaries and the summary of summaries? If they wrote and illustrated an "Illustrated Classic Comic," how does it look? Above all, did your students engage wholeheartedly in the discussion of the book? If you can answer yes to these questions, then you and your students did a good job.

Many sources for classic literature are available on the Internet. Use directories or search engines to generate your own list: Search under "Literature," the names of your favorite authors, or even topics. Sometimes, unfortunately, if you are not a member of a particular Web site, you cannot download the document, but usually this is not a problem. For this reason, you will want to have walked around the Web in search of free, downloadable literature, or be ready to pay. The Gutenberg Project and the Online Book Initiative are excellent sources of public domain literature. Their URLs are listed below.

This strategy takes some planning on your part and you will need to explain it fully. I've found that the first time I use this strategy with a class, the students don't know what to expect. However when I give the students some background information on the book, who the characters are and an inkling of the plot, and then I tell them that they are going to read the book in one or two class periods, they begin to get excited. If the first experience is positive and fun, the students begin to anticipate future experiences. Therefore, the first time you try this strategy, you want to make sure that your goal is attainable. That's another reason why I start with Poe, as the works are not long and the kids tend to like them. After the first positive experience, I assign the Internet search-work to my students, and oftentimes they select the next piece of electronic literature for the class.

Whole Books on the Internet

⬤ Electronic Library

http://www.books.com/scripts/lib.exe

Click on Browse the Electronic Library to find lists of Ancient European Literature, Fiction, Humor, Non-Fiction, Italian Literature, and Poetry.

⬤ The Electronic Text Center at the University of Virginia

http://etext.lib.virginia.edu/english.html

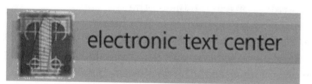

A list of hyperlinks to several hundred books written in English. Click on the Modern English Collection (1500 to Present) and find texts by and about African Americans, Native Americans, women writers, the American Civil War, Thomas Jefferson, Mark Twain. There are also texts for young readers and best sellers from 1900 to 1930.

⬤ Books On-line By Title

http://www-cgi.cs.cmu.edu/cgi-bin/book/maketitlepage

This general collection of literary works, organized by title, is maintained by the library at Carnegie Mellon University. This is a *huge* list of books so, to make it easier to use, go to **http://www.cs.cmu.edu/books.html** where you can do a title, subject or author search.

● The Online Book Initiative

gopher://ftp.std.com:70/11/obi/book

In your browser, type this gopher address to view a list of over 150 authors and categories. There are books by Geoffrey Chaucer and Emily Brontë, by Edgar Allan Poe and Sir Arthur Conan Doyle, from Anglo-Saxon literature to Samuel Clemens, among others. You will be surprised at all there is to read at this one location. With this one site, you will never lack for literature. Remember this is a gopher site, so all you will see is text.

● The Complete Works of William Shakespeare

http://the-tech.mit.edu/Shakespeare/works.html

The works of William Shakespeare are read by most tenth, eleventh, and twelfth graders. The full text of Shakespeare's plays, poems, and sonnets can be downloaded from the MIT Web site. The collection is arranged by category: comedy, history, poetry, tragedy, etc.

● Romantic Circles

http://www.rc.umd.edu/

A Web site devoted to the works of Lord Byron, Mary Wollstonecraft Shelley, Percy Bysshe Shelley, John Keats, their contemporaries and their historical contexts. Click on "electronic editions" or go to **http://www.rc.umd.edu/editions/editions.html** for the texts. This page is not for beginners.

● Women and Literature

http://sunsite.unc.edu/cheryb/women/wlit.html

If your class is interested in women writers, you can find short biographical sketches and works by Louisa May Alcott, Jane Austen, Maya Angelou, Emily Brontë, and Sylvia Plath, plus many others.

⬤ Victorian Women Writers

http://www.indiana.edu/cgi-bin-ip/letrs/vwwplib.pl

A collection of works written by British women writers of the 19th century. The collection keeps growing and now includes over fifty works.

> ## Victorian Women Writers Project

⬤ A Celebration of Women Writers

http://www.cs.cmu.edu/Web/People/mmbt/women/writers.html

This Web site recognizes the contributions of women writers throughout history. You can browse the list by author, century or country.

All of these classical works of literature are on the Internet because their copyright has expired or they are "public domain documents." This means you can copy them and not be violating a copyright agreement. This also means, that most literature found on the Internet was not written within the last twenty years.

Download to your heart's content! Most of it is all still free for the taking—it's like being given an unlimited gift certificate to your favorite bookstore. You will need to establish a storage policy for your class because those hard drives will fill up in no time. If your system includes a spacious server, and every user has a "student locker" in which to save downloaded files, then you are very lucky. If not, it's every kid with a floppy for him- or herself.

"A Book An Hour," has many adaptations. For some content areas, teachers may be able to use a similar process with particularly long chapters in a book, if the topic lends itself to being split up in this fashion. The Internet is one of the greatest libraries around. It never closes, does not require you to return the books, and it levies no fines. What a treat!

Evaluation Rubric for "A Book an Hour"

Assessment Area	Exemplary	Proficient	Not Yet
Summary Construction	• Excellent summary of book segment that is logical and accurate	• Good summary of book that is short but accurate	• Unable to write a short summary • Many factual inaccuracies in the summary
Understanding of the Book	• Summary reflects a very good understanding of the total book as well as the section • Group makes excellent contribution to summary of summaries	• Summary reflects a good understanding of that portion of the book • Group makes simple contribution to summary of summaries	• Summary does not reflect understanding of the book • Group makes small or no contribution to summary of summaries
Classic Comic Edition (optional)	• Graphics and summary enhance the text	• Graphics and summary work well together	• Graphics and summary are not related
Computer and Internet Experience	• Students found Web site for book easily • Students downloaded information easily • Students used knowledge of "multitasking" to write summaries	• Students needed little guidance to find the Web site • Students needed some help in downloading information • Students wrote summaries either by computer or by hand	• Students were unable to find book on line without assistance from others • Students were unable to download information • Students wrote summaries in long hand
Mechanics	• Excellent grammar, punctuation and spelling	• Good grammar, punctuation and spelling	• Faulty grammar, punctuation and spelling
Cooperation	• Students worked well together • Students shared the work load fairly • Students solved problems in a fair manner	• Students worked together with little strife • Burden of work done by small part of the group • Students solved most problems in a fair manner	• Students did not work well together • Burden of work done by one member of the group • Teacher intervention was needed to solve problems

Chapter 14:
Ambassador to Mexico WebQuest

A WebQuest is another type of educational experience that is ideal for the Internet. It is a learning process developed by Bernie Dodge at San Diego State University and has been used by many teachers to date. The December 1996/97 issue of *Classroom Connect* says that "WebQuest" has become one of the buzzwords in educational technology. The lesson for this chapter, The *Ambassador to Mexico WebQuest*, follows the basic template for such a lesson. To find out more about the WebQuest process and to see other WebQuest lessons, please visit the following Web sites:

The WebQuest Page by Bernie Dodge
> **http://edweb.sdsu.edu/webquest/webquest.html**

The WebQuest Design Process by Bernie Dodge
> **http://edweb.sdsu.edu/webquest/Process/**
> **WebQuestDesignProcess.html**

WebQuest Lesson Template for Students
> **http://edweb.sdsu.edu/webquest/LessonTemplate.html**

The WebQuest Page

WebQuestion Lesson Template for Teachers
**http://edweb.sdsu.edu/webquest/
TeacherLessonTemplate.html**

Kathy Schrock's WebQuest Guide
**http://discoveryschool.com/schrockguide/webquest/
webquest.html**

Kathy Schrock's WebQuest Slide Show
**http://discoveryschool.com/schrockguide/webquest/
wqsl1.html**

Generally speaking a WebQuest is a discovery, investigation or inquiry-based activity in which students are to locate information about a topic from the Internet (and other resources such as books, magazines and encyclopedias) to help them develop a presentation. A WebQuest can be either a short-term or long-term project. In either format, it develops analysis and synthesis skills in researching, writing, and presenting. Whether short- or long-term, the students are gathering new knowledge as well as extending their existing knowledge in an area by analyzing and reconstructing a body of information into some kind of an original presentation. A WebQuest should be more than just writing a report, it may include role play, demonstration or simulation. Many of the lessons in this book are good "warm-up" activities for a WebQuest-type lesson. This type of lesson is more sophisticated and should be accomplished when you and your students are ready for a more challenging task. What I've described below is a long-term unit on the study of Mexico.

In Your Classroom

Teacher Template:
Ambassador to Mexico WebQuest

WebQuests generally have two sections. One for the teacher and one for the student. When designing a WebQuest, the teacher needs to choose a topic, identify resources, establish goals, design assessment strategies, specify the task(s) for the students to accomplish, design the lesson, develop Web pages, implement the lesson, and then, after it is completed, evaluate the results and revise it for future use. What follows is the Teacher Template, followed by the Student Template for the WebQuest.

Introduction

(This is written for you, the teacher, to give you an idea of the scope and sequence of the WebQuest.)

This lesson is designed to help your students discover ways to retrieve meaningful information from the Internet. They will become familiar with Mexico by studying its geography, history, politics and government, culture and society, language, archeology and the lives of the children who live there.

In this activity, you are asking your students to be the "advance party" which has been assigned to provide you with a special briefing, since you have just been chosen to be the new Ambassador to Mexico. The "advance party" will be divided into teams, each studying one aspect of Mexico for the purposes of preparing a written report and oral briefing for you, before you leave for your new career. The goal for the "advanced party" is to give you all the information on particular topics about Mexico, so that when you land at the airport you will feel quite knowledgeable.

Content Area and Grade Level Audience; Curriculum Standards

The lesson is designed for the secondary (middle school and high school) social studies class. This lesson reinforces curriculum standards in the areas of history, geography, political science, culture, and archeology, and it gives further practice in communication skills. By the end of the lesson, each team of students will have expertise on one aspect of life in Mexico. From the various briefings, they will also have a more thorough knowledge about our neighbor to the south.

Implementation Overview

You will divide your class into teams of advance parties, each with the task of finding information on one specific topic. Each team will be given a worksheet with important questions that they need to answer and a set of relevant Web sites. They can also add questions and Web sites to the basic set when it becomes necessary to do so. If all goes according to plan, the Ambassador WebQuest should take about three weeks to accomplish. It will take at least three to four class meetings to cover all the worksheet questions. You will need two or three class meetings for each team to work on a written report. During the next two class meetings the teams will begin the preparations for the oral briefing, including role plays, demonstrations, etc., that will be presented to you, the new Ambassador. At the last class meeting(s), the teams will brief the new Ambassador and be prepared to answer any questions that you or other class members have. To make this splashy, you might videotape the briefing section and show it to other classes.

You may want to provide your students with a sample WebQuest unit so they may have a model for this activity. Kathy Schrock's WebQuest page has several lessons for you to show: visit **http:// topcat.bridgew.edu/~kschrock/ED560/ed560.htm**.

Resources Needed

You will need to have the following resources available to teach this lesson:

- Class sets of books on Mexico, including fiction and nonfiction.

- Encyclopedias, atlases, dictionaries, language books.

- Video or audio materials on Mexico.

- Online computers and e-mail accounts for each group of students.

- Appropriate software for 1) online research, 2) word processing, and 3) presentation (if necessary)

- Lists of Web sites for geography, history, political science, culture, language, archeology and children which are bookmarked or cataloged on a Web page.

To accomplish the lesson, you will also need: one social science teacher (and a Spanish teacher if possible); a librarian/media specialist who can help with research; e-mail addresses for people in Mexico who will correspond with your class; if possible a person from Mexico who can help with some questions; and Mexican objects and regalia such as clothes, musical instruments, etc. You might include a field trip to a local museum, if there is one, that has Mexican artifacts that will be helpful to your students.

Entry Level Skills and Knowledge

Your students should be able to do a research project. They will need to search for items on the Web; sift data to find appropriate information; work together as a team; compose e-mail messages; use a word processor; and download information from the Internet, etc. You will have to decide if you want your students to self-select teams, or if you will assign teams. (In the student template below, I have the students self-select teams, a procedure which works for some groups of youngsters, but not for all.)

As a teacher, you will need to have the lesson very well organized. A list of Web sites for the lesson appears in the last section of this chapter. From that list, determine Web sites that each team of students should visit. Develop worksheets to help students stay on task.

Evaluation

Use an evaluation rubric that includes: organization of ideas and content in the written report; organization of ideas and content in the briefing; use of art/graphics, role playing/simulation and demonstrations in the briefing; overall Internet experience and usage; and mechanics and cooperation. You will have to decide if the students on each team will receive a common grade for the written report and briefing or an individual grade. A sample rubric has been included at the end of the chapter.

Possible Variations

I've written a WebQuest which is designed for a unit focusing on Mexico, but this is a basic template that you can use for any country. Also think about other possible WebQuests: "The Pyramids of the World: Egypt and Mexico," "Children Who Have Made A Difference," "Books by Mark Twain," "Women in History," "Ups and Dows: A Stock Market Quest," and the list goes on and on. Any topic with quality Web-based information is a potential subject for a WebQuest.

Conclusion

Upon completing this WebQuest your students should:

- Be an expert on their specific topic.
- Be knowledgeable about other aspects of the country from the presentations they have heard.
- Know how to do research using the library and the Internet.
- Have used their creative and artistic talents.

Bookmarks for the *Ambassador to Mexico WebQuest*

General Web sites on Mexico

Mexico for Kids
http://explora.presidencia.gob.mx/index_kids.html

The Mexican Travel Guide
http://www.go2mexico.com/

Profile of Mexico by the U.S. State Department
http://www.state.gov/www/regions/ara/1mexprof.html

Flags and Maps
http://www.plcmc.lib.nc.us/kids/mow/default.asp
Click on M and scroll to Mexico.

The CIA World Factbook
http://www.odci.gov/cia/publications/factbook/ index.html Click on Country Listing and scroll down to Mexico or go to **http://www.odci.gov/cia/publications/ factbook/mx.html**

Mexico's Index Channel
http://www.trace-sc.com/index1.htm

Mexico Web (in Spanish)
http://mexico.web.com.mx/ (similar to Yahoo)

Translation of Spanish Websites
http://babelfish.altavista.digital.com/cgi-bin/translate?
Type in the URL of the Web site that you want translated, and Babel Fish at AltaVista will try to translate the Web site from Spanish to English. The translation might not be completely accurate and/or "stilted," but it should give your students a general idea of the meaning of the Web site page.

Geography of Mexico

Map of Mexico
> **http://www.lib.utexas.edu/Libs/PCL/Map_collection/ americas/Mexico.GIF**

Map of Mexico from National Geographic
> **http://www.nationalgeographic.com/resources/ngo/ maps/view/images/mexicom.jpg**

Mexico's Geography
> **http://explora.presidencia.gob.mx/pages_kids/ geography/geography_kids.html**

General Information about States in Mexico
> **http://www.mexonline.com/estado.htm**

Yahoo Guide to States in Mexico
> **http://www.yahoo.com/Regional/Countries/Mexico/ States/**

Yahoo Guide to Cities in Mexico
> **http://www.yahoo.com/Regional/Countries/Mexico/ Cities/**

History of Mexico

A Brief History of Mexico
> **http://www.go2mexico.com/history.html**

The Meaning of Cinco de Mayo
> **http://www.kqed.org/fromKQED/Cell/Calhist/cinco.html**

Cinco de Mayo
> **http://latino.sscnet.ucla.edu/demo/cinco.html**

Mexico Timelines
> **http://explora.presidencia.gob.mx/pages_kids/history/ history_kids.html** or **http://www.humanities-interactive.org/splendors/timeline.htm**

Pancho Villa (in Spanish)
> **http://mexico.udg.mx/Historia/Trajes/dorado.html**

Children and Youth of Mexico

Rockeros Mexicano (in Spanish)
http://www.rockeros.com/mex.htm

Intercultural E-Mail Classroom Connections
http://www.stolaf.edu/network/iecc/

Politics and Government in Mexico

The Government of Mexico: The Presidency
http://world.presidencia.gob.mx/

The Government
**http://explora.presidencia.gob.mx/pages_kids/
government/government_kids.html**

President Zedillo
**http://explora.presidencia.gob.mx/pages_kids/
government/president_kids.html**

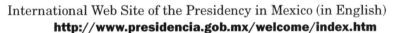

International Web Site of the Presidency in Mexico (in English)
http://www.presidencia.gob.mx/welcome/index.htm

Government and Political Conditions of Mexico
http://www.state.gov/www/regions/ara/3govpol.html

Foreign and U.S. Mexican Relations
http://www.state.gov/www/regions/ara/5fusrel.html

Money, Exchange and Credit
http://www.go2mexico.com/money.html

Culture and Society in Mexico

Culture and Society of Mexico
**http://www.public.iastate.edu/~rjsalvad/scmfaq/
scmfaq.html**

Mexican Holidays
http://www.go2mexico.com/holidays.html

People and History of Mexico
http://www.state.gov/www/regions/ara/2peophis.html

The Burrito Page
http://www.infobahn.com/pages/rito.html

La Cocina Mexicana (Mexican Cuisine) (in English)
http://mexico.udg.mx/cocina/ingles/

Bullfighting in Mexico
http://uxdea1.iimas.unam.mx/~david/index.html
(click on English, frames or no frames for a translation)

Artes e Historia (in Spanish)
http://www.arts-history.mx/museos/muse.html

Language of Mexico

Basic Spanish for the Virtual Student
http://www.umr.edu/~amigos/Virtual/

The Human Languages Page
http://www.june29.com/ (this is a HUGE Web site)

The Spanish Language
http://www.eden.com/~tomzap/spanish.html

Weekly Spanish Lesson
http://www.june29.com//Spanish/lesson1.html

Peoples of Mexico

The Aztec
http://northcoast.com/~spdtom/aztec.html

Mystery of the Maya
http://www.mysteriousplaces.com/
Chichen_Itza_Page.html

Aztecs/Mexicas
http://www.indians.org/welker/aztec.htm

Indigenous Peoples in Mexico
http://www.indians.org/welker/mexman01.htm

Tlahuica Culture of Morelos
http://www.albany.edu/~mesmith/tlahuica.html

Quetzalcoatl: The Man, The Myth, The Legend
http://weber.ucsd.edu/~anthclub/quetzal.htm

Possible questions/problems/concerns for students to respond to (by category)

History

- What are the important dates in the history of Mexico?
- What are important dates for children and youth in the history of Mexico?
- Are there any "famous" or "important" children who helped shape the history of Mexico? If so, what did they do that was important?
- Show pictures of people who are famous in the history of Mexico.
- Find out about and re-enact a famous event that shaped the history of Mexico.

Politics and Government

- Describe the political parties in Mexico. What is the name of dominant political party?
- Who is the President of Mexico? Give background information on him or her.
- Describe the capital city of Mexico. Who is the mayor of Mexico City? Tell some important information about the city and the mayor.
- Write about the current policy issues between Mexico and the United States.
- Describe the North American Free Trade Agreement (NAFTA) and its effect on the United States and Mexico.
- Describe the currency (money) of Mexico and give the exchange rate. Share examples if possible.

Culture and Society (Cultural Anthropology)

- What are some customs of Mexico that the Ambassador will have to know?
- What is the native dress of Mexico? Show pictures of girls, boys, women and men; or if possible, wear an example of the native dress. If there is more than one native dress, give examples from the various regions in Mexico.
- What is the main religion of Mexico? What other religions are practiced? Show pictures of churches, temples and/or places of religious worship.
- What holidays or festivals are important to children and youth? Tell the new Ambassador why these are important.
- Share traditional Mexican food and tell why it's important.
- Share a traditional Mexican dance and talk about its significance.

Language

- What are the languages spoken by the people of Mexico? Give some examples of the main language, as well as phrases that the Ambassador will need to know.

- What are some legends, myths and beliefs of the people of Mexico?
- Share information about the ancient cultures of Mexico and why they are important to the children of Mexico.

Peoples of Mexico

- Give a brief history of the Mayan culture.
- Share pictures and facts about the Mayan people.
- Give a brief history of the Aztec culture.
- Share pictures and facts about the Aztec people.
- Share pictures and facts about other ancient cultures in Mexico.
- Show pictures and facts about three to four important archeological sites.

Children and Youth

- What type of music is popular with the children? Play a recording of a piece of music.
- What types of clothes do teenagers like to wear? Show pictures.
- Find out information about school. How much schooling is required? How many hours a day? Cost of schooling? College education available? Differences between education for girls and boys?
- What role do children play in the family? Types of chores/tasks/jobs children are expected to do? Are children expected to work? If so, what types of jobs do children do?
- What aspirations do Mexican children have when they reach adulthood?
- What are favorite sports or hobbies for children and youth?

The Process

To accomplish this task you will need to do the following:

- Select the team you want to join, then determine a team leader who is responsible for the calendar and seeing that the written report and oral briefing are done on time.
- Select people to answer each of the questions in the six areas.
- Add questions if you think they are necessary for the briefing of the Ambassador.
- All team members are to write a summary page for each Web site visited—and book or article read—that had information on your topic.
- Collate the summaries to create a report that answers each of the questions.
- Draw or copy any important maps or pictures to enhance the report.
- Write the report, edit for clarity and errors, then rewrite the report.
- Develop an oral briefing for your report.
- Collect all articles needed for a role play, demonstration or simulation.
- Collaborate with the other teams to determine the order of presentation.

- Give your oral briefing with examples and/or regalia as needed.
- Take notes on other oral briefings.
- Be prepared to answer any questions the new Ambassador has about your briefing.

Evaluation

You will be evaluated on the following:

- Ideas and content of your written report and/or oral briefing to the Ambassador.
- Organization of the report and briefing.
- Cooperation with your team and the class.
- Art/graphics, demonstrations, role play and simulations you included in the report and briefing.
- Mechanics of your report: spelling, grammar, punctuation, and writing style.

Conclusion

Upon completing this WebQuest you should:

- Be an expert on one of the topics studied on Mexico.
- Be knowledgeable about the geography, history, politics, government, culture and society, archeology and children of Mexico from the briefings.
- Know how to do research using the library and the Internet.
- Have used your creative and artistic talents.

Evaluation Rubric for
"Ambassador to Mexico WebQuest"

Assessment Area	Exemplary	Proficient	Not Yet
Organization of Ideas and Content of the Written Report	• Very good introduction • Ideas are clear • Many details are included • Smooth, easy pace • Good placement of details • Strong conclusion	• Good introduction • Ideas somewhat clear • Some details are included • Some trouble following pace • Some details, but out of order • Good conclusion	• Introduction boring • Hard to read • Wanders aimlessly • Stops abruptly or drags on • Unclear ideas • Details broad, general and vague
Organization of Ideas and Content of the Briefing	• Excellent pacing of briefing • Briefing follows written presentation • Briefing includes role plays, simulations and/or demonstrations • Group answers all questions posed by other students or the new Ambassador	• Good pacing of briefing, (few time lags) • Briefing wanders a little from written presentation • Briefing includes only one role play, simulation or demonstration • Group can respond to most questions posed to them	• Pacing of briefing is slow • Briefing disorganized and does not follow written report • Briefing does not include any role play, simulation or demonstration • Group cannot respond to most questions posed by other students
Use of Art/Graphics, Role Play, Simulation, and Demonstrations in the Briefing	• Reflects research • Follows a detailed plan • Carefully and neatly done • Art/graphics are an asset to the text • Role play adds important information to briefing • Demonstrations are well organized	• Reflects some research • Shows some planning • Mostly done carefully and neatly • Art/graphics aid the text • Role play is pertinent to briefing • Demonstrations are organized	• Does not reflect research • Is not planned • Is not done carefully and neatly • Art/graphics harmful to text • Role play is disorganized • Demonstrations are not relevant to briefing
Mechanics	• Excellent grammar, punctuation and spelling • Easy to read aloud	• Good grammar, punctuation and spelling • Most parts easy to read	• Faulty grammar, punctuation and spelling • Awkward to read out loud
Cooperation	• Students worked well together • Students shared the work load fairly • Students solved problems in a fair manner	• Students worked together with little strife • Burden of work done by small part of the group • Students solved most problems in a fair manner	• Students did not work well together • Burden of work done by one member of the group • Teacher intervention was needed to solve problems

Chapter 15:
The Games People Play

You were probably thinking that your kids already spend too much time playing computer games, and that if they would only invest some of that time on studying, they would corner the market of electronic knowledge. Face it! Kids play. In fact as many educational theorists have stated, play is kids' work, so why not show them some good, clean, healthy electronic playgrounds on the Internet! That, alas, is easier said than done. All kinds of games on the Internet are available to everyone, but even games that may at first blush look like they're OK for kids, may eventually cause a lot of blushing.

As with arcade games at the mall, some of the games on the Internet are violent and gory, sexually explicit, or filled with language that is too vulgar. A few sites rely on chance: You can play a virtual slot machine, poker, or blackjack on the Internet. You can also test your knowledge of beer trivia and take a short course in wine savvy. If you do not want your kids visiting these Web sites, then you will not want to put an all-inclusive games list in your bookmark collection. You will want to be more selective, perhaps compiling your own collection, steering the kids away from the games of which you disapprove by steering them towards the games that you do approve. If your students have been to games sites at home, you can be sure they will visit the same Web sites at school.

Our role, as Internet-using teachers, is threefold: 1) To establish standards that we think are appropriate for our classrooms (and school and community); 2) To check out the Internet sites that our students might visit to make sure that they meet our standards; and 3) To explain and uphold our standards with our students, engaging them in discussion to help them understand our point of view and assisting them in learning to discriminate the appropriate from the inappropriate. If your students are misusing the Internet in your classroom, then you need to take action. For that, you know what needs to be done far better then I do.

This might be a good time to remind them about your Acceptable Use Policy or AUP. We talked about it in Chapter 4. Remember what was agreed upon in your AUP and enforce it. If you are using an Internet Driver's License, this is a good time to see if your students are driving down the information superhighway safely, wisely and well.

While playing games might not be the first thing you want your students to be doing in class, they can learn several things by working with games. Other than thinking skills and motor coordination skills, they will learn how to download FTP files. Many games are large, so they have been compressed and placed at FTP sites on the Internet. Thus, if your students download a game, they get practice at using FTP procedures. They also get practice using decompression and virus checking programs, installing the files on a hard drive and then deciphering the game's set up. This is a procedure that can be transferred to downloading other types of files and programs.

Then, there is the issue of "multiple intelligences." According to Howard Gardner, among the seven frames of mind people have, there are logical-mathematical and bodily-kinesthetic folks. Students with these intelligences love games: mind games and physical games, respectively. In addition, game sites do reinforce thinking skills, and sometimes reading, writing and arithmetic.

So Many Games

That said, let's go ahead and look at a general games list so that you can be knowledgeable about what's out there. Then glean from the general list the games that you think will be interesting and appropriate. Start to build your own selected games list for availability to your class on your bookmark collection. You might want to have a "games" recess for your students. I've listed a few "child safe" game sites that have some teaching/learning merit. If you are interested in other types of games for kids, check out Yahooligans and click on Computers and Games. From there go to Online Games and see selections for chess, coloring, interactive stories, math, mazes, puzzles, word games, sport games and trivia. I like Yahooligans because the links will be to child-safe game sites on the Web. One of the maze Web sites leads to the AMazeGame at **http://www.wenet.net/users/rpaymer/**.

Family Friendly Games at **http://www.familygames.com/ index.html** is a collection of games that you can download before you decide to buy them. The .com says this is a commercial site. Every game at this SafeSurf-approved site is designed with kids and learning in mind. If you worry about violence, this is one location where there is a bunch of non-violent shareware and freeware games for Windows (sorry Mac folks).

Bill Kendrick's Web site **http://www.billsgames.com/home.html** has a collection of free Web-based games for the whole family. You can download card games such as solitaire, play video poker and slider, board games like Tic-Tac-Toe and Connect 4, word games like Hangman (with a selection of dictionaries from easy to difficult), "Plaid Libs," and brain teasers. You can also download

mazes. Beware, this page is time consuming and lots of fun for everyone.

Alive Software Games and Education at **http://www.alivesoft.com/** offers free downloads for PC users of their various games that reinforce thinking skills and strategy. Each game has a short introduction and a link to click to download the game.

For "kid-oriented games" go to Fish in Space **http:// www.jaked.org/**. This site has a Magic 8 Infinity-ball for predicting the future, as well as an easy-to-use game of Tic-Tac-Toe. There are three modes of play: very easy, easy, and hard. You can choose to be either the X or the O. This is an excellent game of strategy and sportsmanship, and your kids do have to think to make T-T-T work. A more difficult version of Tic-Tac-Toe is the three dimensional variety at **http://www.hepl.phys.nagoya-u.ac.jp/cgi-bin/3dttt**. This Web site offers no directions for getting the game to start, but it's easy: point and click, then wait for the computer to make a move, and then point and click again. The red and blue "stones" will appear magically on the screen before you. The game keeps a winner's list of the names of people who have been successful at it.

At Boston College's **http://www.bu.edu/Games/games.html**, you can play several logic games that pit you against a computer. The computer usually wins. The Peg Game, Tic-Tac-Toe, Minesweep, Hunt the Wumpus, and 9 Puzzle are non-Java games. They also have Java versions of Battleship and 9 Puzzle. The Java games are faster than the non-Java games, but you must have a browser that supports Java. If you want to see what Java enhancement can do for a game, compare a Java game with a non-Java game. There really is a difference in speed and "mouse-ability" in the Java version, because the program is running on your machine, rather than a Boston College Web server.

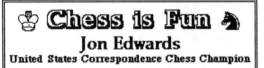

Jon Edwards
United States Correspondence Chess Champion

Chess games abound on the Internet. To learn the basics of chess go to Chess is Fun at **http://www.princeton.edu/~jedwards/cif/chess.html**. If you want to play chess on the Web go to WebChess at **http://www.june29.com/Chess/** or GNUWebChess at **http://www.delorie.com/game-room/chess/**. There are many, many more chess games online. I wish I could give you more information about which site is the best, but this is one game I've never been able to get into. This is one of my many shortcomings. What can I say?

If you want to download games to your own or the class computer, bear in mind my warnings. For one thing, the sites are slow because of all the graphics.. While these Web sites contain child-safe games, there are other game sites on the Internet that do not. In your searches, if you find a game that is too violent or otherwise inappropriate, my advice is the old saying, "Pick the roses and leave the thorns."

You can also devise your own games using online resources. You can also invent computer-aided games based on tried-and-true classroom games that have been used for eons.

For example, I developed an Anticipation Game that was based on a Web site relating to a subject one of "my" classes was studying (I work in many classrooms during the year). The Anticipation Game teaches the students better use of a search engine or directory, as well as the Find button (which searches for a chosen word on a Web page) in Netscape. It also reinforces reading skills through skimming and scanning, and writing skills. To make the game work, you need a Web site with links to other pages. Luckily, Web sites like these are readily available on just about any subject area you can think of and a few are listed in other chapters of this book. You can do an InfoSeek Search on "Bosnia" and come up with a least ten Web sites that might be useful for this type of game. Select the one you think is best for your purposes.

This Anticipation Game was devised for a fifth-grade class that was studying the solar system. It was one of the last assignments to be accomplished during the three-week unit. It is an activity that two students work on together. It does not need an evaluation rubric as the correct answers are evident. The kids seem to like this type of activity. I like it too, as it reinforces what has been studied in the class while offering new pieces of information in a painless way. If you are sneaky, you can create questions that involve higher-order thinking skills, as well as creativity, to answer. This adds to the challenge.

This Anticipation Game has two parts: First, the players have to locate a usable Web site; and second, they have to anticipate the answer to the question before checking out their answer on the Web site. By the way, you can find the answers to this Anticipation Game at The Nine Planets home page on **http://seds.lpl.arizona.edu/billa/tnp/**.

If you want the answers without resorting to the Web, here they are 1) Pluto; 2) Earth; 3) Aphelion [point where the object is farthest from the Sun]; 4) Saturn, Jupiter, Neptune and Uranus have rings; 5) It's the largest mountain in our solar system; 6) Jupiter; 7) Earth; 8) False—asteroids are small rocky bodies and comets are small icy bodies; 9) They both have an orbit, they both revolve around the sun, and they are both named after characters in Roman Mythology; and 10) Jovian, Terrestrial and Pluto.

The first time you play the Anticipation Game, model the game for your students. As your students become more adept at the game, make the questions more demanding. In addition, teams of students can make up Anticipation Games on other Web sites and topics of study, for other folks in the class to play. That way, they learn both when they are inventing the game and when they play it. Here are some other great Web sites that lend themselves well to the Anticipation Game:

Castles on the Web
http://www.castlesontheweb.com/

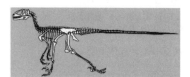

Dinosauria OnLine
http://www.dinosauria.com/

The Maya Astronomy Page
http://www.astro.uva.nl/~michielb/maya/astro.html

The Sun Page
http://www.hao.ucar.edu/public/education
education.html#additional.haoh_edu

A simpler, easier computer-aided game that you can play with your students using the Internet is a kind of Scavenger Hunt. Download a short story or poem from an appropriate site on the Internet (or require the game-player to download the file), put it in a file with a number of questions about the text, and require that the game-player find each item in the scavenger hunt. For Web sites with good stories and poems, check out some of the sites in Chapter 2.

I've always loved the imagery in "Jabberwocky," by Lewis Carroll. The Jabberwocky Variations Web site at **http://www.pobox.com/ ~keithlim/jabberwocky/** has many translations and parodies as well as the poem itself. Here is a scavenger hunt that I devised for "Jabberwocky":

I. Read "Jabberwocky," by Lewis Carroll, at http://www.pobox.com/~keithlim/ jabberwocky/
II. Respond to the following items based on "Jabberwocky,"
- Draw a Jabberwock.
- Create a new action word for the Jabberwock to do. Define the word and draw a picture of the Jabberwock doing it.
- Define slithy? Why do you want be slithy? Argue your case.
- Pick out another word in the poem. Define it. Why would you not want one? Argue your case.

- Why should you beware the bandersnatch? What will happen if you are not cautious of one?
- What type of sword is a "vorpel sword?" Describe it to the best of your ability.
- Read two or three of the parodies of Jabberwocky and with a partner see if you can write a Jabberwocky parody too.

Jabberwocky Variations

Games—let them have their place in your online classroom! They serve more purposes than just diversion, comic relief, relaxation or reward. Games teach us to be logical and precise and strategic in our thinking. Games can serve to reinforce skills and knowledge that you have been teaching. Maybe that's the best part—the kids learn, have fun while they're doing it, and don't even notice that they are learning. That's winning the best game of all, the Teacher Game!

Anticipation Game: The Solar System

Names: _____   Date: _____

Part I:

Find a Web site with many links about the Solar System to help you answer the questions.

http:// _____

Title: _____

Part II

Write your best guess, then check the Web site to see if it is correct.

My Anticipated Answer	The Question	Correct Answer & URL
	What is the smallest planet in our Solar System?	
	Which has the larger diameter: Earth or Mars?	
	What is the opposite of *perihelion*?	
	Name at least two planets with rings.	
	Why is the *Olympus Mons* an important feature on Mars?	
	What planet is the fourth brightest object in the sky?	
	Many planets are named for Greek or Roman gods or heroes. Which ones are not?	
	True or false: Comets and Asteroids are the same. Why or why not?	
	Name three things that Venus and Neptune have in common.	
	Describe the three types of planets found in our Solar System.	

Chapter 16:
Just for the
Little Kids

A colleague of mine has a seven-year-old and a 23-month-old. The seven-year-old is already a computer whiz: He plays games, does his own Internet searches for more games, is knowledge-able about both hardware and software, and is doing homework on the family computer. His little brother had mostly been watching.

One hot day, when mother and sons came home from a grocery-shopping expedition, the 23-month-old imperiously commanded: "'Puter, Mommy! 'Puter!" "In a minute, honey!" my friend replied, wiping the melting ice cream off her elbow.

Impatient, the younger sibling scrambled up the stairs to the computer room, and in a few seconds, my friend heard the "Ding!" that told her that someone had turned on the computer. "He can't hurt it or himself," she thought, and finished putting the grocer-ies away, and then forgot all about it. Thirty minutes later, she remembered—stillness in a house full of kids is a loud warning. Up the stairs she went.

The less-than-two-year-old had turned on the switch at the surge protector, negotiated the main menu, found the game he wanted, and was now blissfully wrapped up in 'puter play.

What 3- to 8-year-olds can do with the Internet

How young can they learn? It's a question of motor control, not of mind—the mind is ready to learn at birth (and, some would say, before birth). For you, the point is this: Your kids are probably already inherently better at computers than you are because they are younger, naturally meddlesome, full of curiosity, and many of them grew up in a world where these machines are as familiar as TVs, whereas you did not. More importantly, their minds are like a whole roll of expensive paper towels: They can soak up almost as much as you can pour on them. Have no hesitation about presenting sophisticated Internet instruction to even your youngest students. What they can't execute on their own, they can watch and learn from, and they can understand just about anything you tell them, if you use words that they know or can guess. In other words, they are the online generation and we are not!

Please don't misunderstand me. I love books (basic organizers of offline knowledge) and the enjoyment they bring, but I also know that if my students are going to be ready for the 21st century job market, they have to know how to work with online computers. To that end, start them as early as possible, assuming you feel comfortable with the idea.

The Internet is full of ideas and possibilities for 3-4-5-6-7- to 8-year-olds, not to mention 23-month-olds: stories, games, pictures, and just the sheer fascination of watching the world blip and bleep on a screen before their eyes. Just as Sesame Street gave a whole generation a head start with reading readiness, the kids raised with computer games are going to be ahead in terms of a variety of skills: small motor control in their fingers, hierarchical logic (finding their way with menus and through Web sites), spelling (one has to be precise when keying in URLs), and keyboard writing readiness (it's easier to type, once you know how, than it is to wield a pen or pencil). There are traditional skills that can benefit from use of the Internet too. These include left-to-right reading orientation, letter and picture recognition skills, vocabulary development, and reading and writing skills.

In a national study done by the Center for Applied Technology (October, 1996), it was found that students who know how to use technology are better independent, critical thinkers, can find information more readily, and are better able to manage and present information. Linda Roberts from the Department of Education says that "technology is a tool to help us improve learning opportunities for our students."

Little people can walk the Internet, drive the search engines, download the files, and play the games just like big people, though they may need a bit more guidance. You probably will not have all your little people working with the Internet on a daily basis, but my guess is that you will find them eager to log on. As the story of my friend and her not-quite-two-year-old indicates, kids and computers are natural allies. If you have an online computer in your classroom, there's no reason for it not to be in use by someone all the time. Getting some of them to leave it alone will be a bigger problem than getting most of them interested in it! So, even in kindergarten and the primary grades, make the Internet an integral part of your curriculum; it can teach so much and with so little effort or stress.

One problem you will confront is the age-old problem of the haves and the have-nots. Some young kids have computers at home, and they will come to your class already computer literate and ready to log on. Others not only will not have computers at home, they might not know the joys of reading a book. In our time, the computer have-nots are seriously at risk in the scramble for knowledge, and it is your job as a teacher in a democracy to help make computer equality a new amendment to the Constitution. To this end there is E-Rate (**http://www.ed.gov/Technology/ eratemenu.html**) which is the President's commitment to bring technology into the classroom. Check it out to see if your school can qualify for technology discounts.

Computers belong in the primary grades

Right now, I'm seeing kindergartners coming to school who already know how to operate a computer. They can turn it on and off, identify letters on the keyboard, and use rudimentary hunt-and-peck typing skills to access and work on the programs that they know. Your students who have this much skill can also access the Internet. Your other students will need your help to catch up, but if you give it to them, they will catch up fast. I see them playing reading and math games from CD-ROMs and they are able to explain what they are learning when asked.

The computer in and of itself is an excellent resource for teaching left-to-right reading orientation (a desperately needed corrective against the evil effects of watching too much television), symbol-to-letter recognition, sound-to-symbol recognition, and word-to-symbol recognition. On the other hand, not all grown-ups like computers, and neither—you may be sure—do all kids. Children whose "frame of mind" is dominantly bodily-kinesthetic (as Howard Gardner might put it) may have trouble sitting still for computer time. Let's not make the mistake that has been made so often in the past: This online technology, though it may be the best thing since sliced bread to you or me, is not as appealing to some children as it is to others, and it will not work equally well for all. (Not everyone likes sliced bread, either.)

Internet work is trickier with little ones, but not impossible. Peer collaboration is one excellent way to go: Work with a teacher in an upper grade, and set up a couple of times in the week for your little folks to partner with the older kids. To make maximum use of the available computers, some of your kids could go to the other room, and some of the other kids could come to your room. With this computer-buddy system—one little kid and one big kid (or two and two around a single computer, taking turns)—your students can walk the Web, see exciting Web sites, read files, compose e-mail, download programs, games and files, carry on a keypal correspondence with someone overseas (or across town), and compose their own literary masterpieces.

See Chapter 7, "E-pals and Keypals," for addresses of mailing lists that specialize in electronic penpals, even for the little folks. You can view Kid's Com at **http://www.kidscom.com/** where your students can sign up for penpals or send an electronic card to a friend. By the way, like most sites in this chapter, it is "Kid Safe." There is even a special place for "mousers" (kids who cannot type) with audio prompts and great learning activities. If you are interested, go to **http://www.kidscom.com/orakc/Mousers/ mouse.html**.

When you involve your students in an e-mail activity, they will begin to communicate with one another on a plane quite different from the ordinary. E-mail gives adults instant intimacy and an ability to work together without knowing one another well. I do not know what goes on in the minds of little kids as they face a screen with a message on it from their peers, but an equally powerful mental alchemy is at work, and it is good. At the least, the e-mail experience seems to help little people negotiate their way out of their ego-centered stage in kindergarten and first grade and start thinking about, and with, others.

Take a look at the e-mail books a group of second graders are publishing at Hoffer Elementary School and Murphy Ranch School. Both are accessible at **http://cmp1.ucr.edu/exhibitions/ hoffer/home/hoffer.e-mail.html**.

In situations where the younger student knows what to say but has insufficient skills to write it down, the older student can do the writing or typing. Taking dictation from the younger buddy is good writing practice for the older buddy, and, then, reading the printout will prove to be an altogether inspiring "language-experience" for the not-yet-quite-literate author.

This approach is good for both sets of kids for more reasons than just teaching them computer skills. The bigger kids learn about patience, along with listening, asking, clarifying, helping, and giving feedback, not to mention typing, spelling, grammar, and reading skills. (Reassure the older peer tutors that they can ask you for help, if they get stuck.) The littler kids learn how to compose their thoughts and dictate them in a logical manner, how to answer questions intelligently, how to correct an older person thoughtfully, and how rationally to get what they want. Both ages of kids learn how to get along with one another.

After your students have worked with e-mail and are comfortable with their cyber-buddies, they can venture out onto the Internet together. At first, I thought FTP was too difficult for 6-year-olds. That notion lasted until I saw home pages that had been made by young children! These kids have set up home pages incorporating their own stuff and documents from all over the Internet.

PeanutNet

There are many home pages on the Web authored by kids and/or their parents. (It's difficult to tell who is doing the coding.) Since Web resources are read-point-and-click interfaces, they are not technologically difficult for youngsters to access. Recent Web browsers have graphics and sound capabilities that make them ideal for younger kids. Computers equipped with audio software and sound and video cards make the Web just that much more appealing to kids. Many of the Web pages created by kids have sound and QuickTime movies, and all of them have links to other Web sites. Here are a couple of the many home pages created by or for little people.

● Emma Bowen's Home Page

http://www.comlab.ox.ac.uk/oucl/users/jonathan.bowen/children/emma.html

Emma regularly updates her Web site, and I've been reading it for five years. I've seen Emma grow up. She lives in Oxford, England, with her mother, father and sister. See her stories and pictures. It's quite entertaining.

● Kids Did This

http://sln.fi.edu/tfi/hotlists/kids.html

This hot link collection of kid-generated stuff starts out with this warning: "It's a challenge to keep up with kids on the Internet, but we're trying. Our hotlist of student-produced stuff became too long for one page! Explore the topics that interest you. One word of caution: Some student-designed pages take extra time to load. Caveat surfer."

● The International Kids Space

http://www.kids-space.org/

You can read stories written by kids, view their paintings, ask a doctor for advice, or switch languages from English to Japanese. The youthful authors proclaim their "page is rated G," and it is.

Internet for little guys

The Web is icon-oriented, which makes pointing and clicking easy for beginners. If you have some bookmarks to sites of high interest already loaded, that will make the process easier still. Many Web sites are quite graphical, with pictures and brief explanations that are relatively self-explanatory.

● Theodore Tugboat

http://www.cochran.com/theodore/ and
http://www.pbs.org/tugboat/

If you have seen the popular children's TV program, Theodore Tugboat, then you know what to expect. At this Web site you can enjoy the interactive storybook with pictures, the coloring book, and the hot links to other places kids like to go on the Internet. The page has RealAudio so you can listen to it now. You can view the mirror site from PBS online.

● PBS Kids Online

http://www.pbs.org/kids/

PBS is a great resource for kids too. Click on Fun and Games, Babble On, TV sites and Preschool for songs, coloring, pictures and stories that are very interesting, entertaining and full of good learning.

● Coloring Books

http://coloring.com/

There are many coloring books on the Web—this is just one of them. Just click on a color and on a "spot" on the picture and "voila" that space is colored. If you want to send your creation to someone, you may do so via e-mail. If you want to print out pages in a coloring book for real "crayon" coloring, you can go to Jan Brett's Coloring Pages at **http://www.janbrett.com/ activities_pages_artwork.htm**.

Children's Stories on the Web

Some Web sites are written for children. There are many Web sites that feature children's literature, and I've only listed a few. Luckily, each of these Web sites has links to other sources of online children's literature.

⬤ Children's Story Books Online

http://www.magickeys.com/books/

Possibly the best of the story sites on the Web. There are stories to read and to listen to; a coloring book, riddles and mazes too.

⬤ The IPL Story Hour

http://ipl.sils.umich.edu/youth/StoryHour/

Part of the Internet Public Library Web site, it has links to several stories you can read aloud to your kids. You might want to check out the Main Index for the Youth IPL at **http://ipl.sils.umich.edu/youth/index.html** while you are in the vicinity.

⬤ Children's Stories

http://www.his.com/~pshapiro/stories.menu.html

These are stories written by an elementary school teacher for his students. I especially like the whimsical story about freeze dried water!

⬤ Kidtropolis

http://www.wrightgroup.com/kidtropolis/index.html

Part of The Wright Group publishers, this Web site lets kids create an ending for a story, post a daily news bulletin or talk to an author.

● Simon Says

http://www.simonsays.com/kids/

Go here for the "coolest books on the planet" at least that is what the Web site claims. At this Web site, you need to read the book, then click on the picture of the book for a game type quiz. It's fun!

● Story Creations

http://www.searsportrait.com/storybook/index.html

The folks at Sears have a storybook online that you and your kids can personalize. There are stories for all seasons and places. Because there is RealAudio at the Web site, you can hear the story you have created too.

Internet Favorites of Kids

Since even before Jurassic Park and Barney, dinosaurs have long been a favorite of most primary-age students. On several lists of "kids' favorites" and "what's cool for kids," are Dinosaur Web sites.

● Zoom Dinosaurs

http://www.zoomdinosaurs.com/

This is a large hypertext notebook about dinosaurs. Kids of all ages can use it and learn from it! Find out everything about dinosaurs from their age to their teeth, and lots of stuff in between.

● Dinosauria Online

http://www.dinosauria.com/

This is not a Web site for beginners, but that has not stopped a lot of kids from looking at it. They like the pictures and by the end of the tour they know that dinosaurs are birds!

⬤ The Dinosaur Tour at the Field Museum

http://www.fmnh.org./exhibits/dino/Triassic.htm

It is informative and interesting, with text and graphics. Check it out and judge for yourself whether it's right for your kids. If you decide to teach your primary students using the Dinosaur Home page, I'd be curious to know how it went. Send me some e-mail to **cotton@instruction.com**.

⬤ The Froggy Page

http://frog.simplenet.com/froggy/

Besides big things like dinosaurs, little kids also like small, wiggly things. This Web site is just right for kids who love frogs. It has links to scads of frog-type documents, graphics, fun things to do, and even coloring pages. If you want to delight your six- to eight-year-old herpetologists, click and point them to The Froggy Page.

⬤ Explore the Internet with Dr. I

http://www.ipl.org/youth/DrInternet/

A great site for science-minded kids who want to know more about science and math, as well as the Internet. Dr. I is part of the Internet Public Library.

⬤ The International Museum of the Horse

http://www.imh.org/

I would be remiss if I did not mention this Web site. It has links to information about horses, and young horse lovers think it's great!

A site for kids and parents to share together

Parents and Children Together Online features read-along stories and articles for parents (or teachers) and kids, ages 4–10 to share, along with book reviews and recent children's literature. The free online magazine can be found at the Web site of the ERIC Clearinghouse on Reading, English, and Communication (ERIC/REC): **http://www.indiana.edu/~eric_rec/fl/ras.html**.

Quick and Easy Ways to Get Your kids Published on the Web

Because the archival capacity of virtual space on the Internet is practically infinite, and amazingly inexpensive, for the most part, all the old constraints and cautions of the hard-copy publishing world are now outmoded. Now, everyone who wants to can get published electronically, and if you can't find a place that looks just right to place your electronic publications, you can set up your own electronic publishing company by merely saying you have done so on your own home page. Your class can set up its own home page (see Chapter 4, "Developing and Designing Web Pages") and publish whatever you and your students want. If your class goes into the publishing business, you will want do so with the support of your school. Schools are accountable for the electronic publications of their students, just as they are for other kinds of school publications, so I advise you to talk to the person at your school who knows about such journalistic guidelines. At the Web site below, your kids are welcome to publish their own stories, and they can read stories published by other kids.

● KidsPub

http://www.kidpub.org/kidpub/

Here you can read over 30,000 stories written by kids. To submit a story follow the directions at **http://www.kidpub.org/kidpub/howto.html**.

You and your students can see what other kids are doing in school. Encouraging and empowering, KidsPub is proof that little people can and do write good stories and get them published.

Home Schoolers on the Web

The Internet is also useful for home schoolers. There are many Web sites for home schoolers, take a look at just a few of them. Each has links to other home school Web sites, so you should not have any trouble finding things for your kids to do on the Internet. By the way, there are some good links for children on these pages, too.

● The Teel Home Education Page

http://www.teelfamily.com/education/

Part of a larger site by the Teel Family of Alaska (**http://www.teelfamily.com/**). This page is updated regularly, as the Teel Family is home schooling their children and using the Internet as a means of giving and receiving information.

● Idaho Home School on the Web

http://netnow.micron.net/~ihs/

Resources and information on how to home school your child. Also, you'll find some good curriculum and educational resources.

Other sites besides these are available for young kids, but we could use many more such sites. This is a ripe opportunity for you and your class to take on the project of developing your own Web site, going into the electronic publishing business, and linking up with anything that interests your 4- to 8-year-old students. Cyber-buddies, older with younger, can collaborate to design, code, test, and upload a school home page with individual home pages for each of the grades or for multiple rooms. See Chapter 5 for how to get started on your own home page.

So much is possible using the Internet to teach and learn. Here's a couple more ideas:

- Form a Cyber-Literature Circle by reading and discussing (on e-mail) books with another class online. You can link your class with one down the hall, across town, or on the other side of the globe.

- Go to *The Froggy Page* and develop a lesson by hotlinking to frog fables and frog stories on other pages, all of which can be integrated by linking to yet another page about frog habitat, all of which can be given a scientific bent by linking to the Virtual Frog Dissection Kit. With this kind of electronic leapfrogging, you could hotlink an excellent Frog Unit together!

As with every other chapter in this book, I appreciate your feedback and suggestions. Have you found any other good Web sites for computer whizzes in the twenty-three-month-old to the eight-year-old range? I'd love to hear from you. Please write me at cotton@instruction.com. Thank you!

I hope you have enjoyed reading this book. I wish you many happy hours of Web-walking with *The Online Classroom: Teaching with the Internet.*

Selected Internet Books

Arntson, L. Joyce, Kathy Berkemeyer, Kenn Halliwell, and Thom Neuburger (1998). *Learning the Internet.* 2nd edition. New York: DDC Publishing.

Barrett, Daniel (1997). *Netresearch: Finding Information Online* (Songline Guides). Sebastapol, California.: O'Reilly & Associates.

Burgstahler, Sheryl (1998). *New Kids on Net: A Tutorial for Teachers, Parents and Students.* Boston: Allyn & Bacon.

Burns, Joe (1998). *HTML Goodie.* Indianapolis: MacMillan.

Buyens, Jim (1997). *Running Microsoft Frontpage 98 with CD-ROM.* Austin, TX: Microsoft Press.

Castro, Elizabeth (1999). *HTML 4 for the World Wide Web: Visual QuickStart Guide.* 3rd edition. Berkeley, CA: Peachpit Press.

Comer, Douglas E. (1997). The Internet Book: Everything You Need to Know about Computer Networking and How the Internet Works. 2nd edition. New jersey: Prentice Hall Computer Books.

Condon, William, Butler, Wayne (1997). *Writing the Info Superhighway.* Boston: Allyn & Bacon. ($35.75)

Cotton, Eileen Giuffré (1998). *The Online Classroom: Teaching with the Internet.* 3rd edition. Bloomington, Ind.: ERIC/EDINFO Press.

Family Computer Workshop Staff, ed. (1998). *The Parents' Pocket Guide to Kids and Computers: Top 100 Kids' Software Titles, Top 100 Fun and Safe Internet Sites.* Washington, DC: Family Computer Workshop.

Forta, Ben, and Bryan Gambrel (1999). *Sams Teach Yourself Homesite 4 in 24 Hours* (The Sam Teach Yourself in 24 Hours Series). With CD-ROM. Indianapolis, Ind.: Sams.

Friday, Jennifer, and Chris Mansfield (1998). *101 Cool Sites for Kids on the Internet.* Instruct F.

Glossbrenner, Alfred, and Emily Glossbrenner (1997). *Search Engines for the World Wide Web: Visual Quickstart Guide* (Visual Quickstart Guide Series). Berkeley, Calif.: Peachpit Press.

Gralla, Preston (1999). *Online Kids: A Young Surfer's Guide to Cyberspace.* 2nd edition. New York: John Wiley & Sons.

Gralla, Preston, and Mina Reimer (1998). *How the Internet Works.* New Jersey: Que Education & Training.

Heide, Ann, Linda Stilborne, and Ann Heidi (1999). *The Teacher's Complete & Easy Guide to the Internet.* 2nd edition, with CD-ROM. New York: Teachers College Press.

Hughes, Donna Rice, with Pamela Campbell (1998). *Kids Online: Protecting Your Children in Cyberspace.* Grand Rapids, Mich.: Baker/Revell.

Ideal Instructional Fair, ed. (1999). *Cyberspace for Kids: 600 Sites That Are Kid Tested and Parent-Approved Grades 1–2.* Grand Rapids, Mich.: Instructional Fair/TS Denison.

Kraynak, Joe (1998). *Easy Internet: See It Done, Do It Yourself.* 3rd edition. (Que's Easy Series). New Jersey: Que Education & Training.

Krupnick, Karen, and Kelly Kennedy (1997). *Kids@School.on.the.Net: Fun-Filled Internet Activities Across The Curriculum Plus Exciting Internet Treasure Hunts Grades 3–6.* Santa Barbara, Calif.: The Learning Works.

Miller, Michael (1998). *The Lycos Personal Internet Guide.* New Jersey: QUE Education and Training.

Moran, Barbara, and Kathy Ivens (1998). *Internet Directory for Kids and Parents with CD-ROM.* Foster City, Calif.: IDG Books Worldwide.

Morton, Jessica G. (1998). *Kids on the 'Net: Conducting Internet Research in K–5 Classrooms.* New Hampshire: Heinemann.

Niederst, Jennifer, and Richard Koman, eds. (1998). *Web Design in a Nutshell: A Desktop Quick Reference.* Sebastapol, California.: O'Reilly & Associates.

Polly, Jean Armour (1998). *The Internet Kids and Family Yellow Pages.* 3rd edition. New York: McGraw-Hill Companies.

Segaller, Stephen (1998). *Nerds 2.0.1: A Brief History of the Internet.* New York: TVBooks.

Sonnenreich, Wes, and Tim MacInta (1998). *Web Developer.Com Guide to Search Engines.* New York: John Wiley & Sons.

Vega, Denise (1998). *Learning the Internet for Kids: A Voyage to Internet Treasures.* New York: DDC Publishing.

Want, Robert S., and Jennifer M. Dowell (1998). *Getting Your Child Started on the Internet: A Quick-Reference Guide for Parents and Kids Ages 4 to 12.* New York: Want Publishing Company.

Abridged Glossary of Internet Terms

Acceptable Use Policy (AUP)

A policy addressed to Internet users, aimed at insuring appropriate behavior in cyberspace, and limiting the type of material that can be accessed from the Internet. Enforcement of AUPs varies with the Internet Service Provider. See Chapter 5.

Back

A button on the toolbar which allows you to revisit locations.

Bandwidth

A word used to describe how much data can be sent through a network connection. Plain text documents don't need a lot of bandwidth; movies do.

Bookmarks (Netscape)

A browser function which allows you to keep a list of interesting sites, so they may be easily found again.

Boolean Search

A method of searching for information in databases that combines search terms with the five common Boolean operators: and, or, not, parentheses and "quotation marks."

Browser

An Internet navigation program that interprets and displays hypertext documents. Netscape Navigator and Internet Explorer are examples of browsers. See Chapter 1.

Cache (Netscape)

A location in computer hard-disk memory where data is stored for easy retrieval.

Cookie

A short file put on your system by a Web page, which includes information about your usage, and makes the current interaction happen. For example, it may include the information that you have already logged into a password area during the current session, and don't need a second password check. There are many uses for cookies. They may be erased at the end of a session, or kept until the next session, and they may be written in code or in plain text.

CU-SeeMe

Pronounced "See you, See me," it is a publicly available video-conferencing program developed at Cornell University. If you have audio/video capabilities, and an Internet connection, you can videoconference with someone else with the same capabilities. It also allows many people to videoconference at the same time.

Cyberspace

Term originated by author William Gibson in his novel *Neuromancer*. Cyberspace, the Internet, and the Information Superhighway are considered synonyms.

Directories

See Search Engines.

Domain Name System (DNS)

The Internet naming scheme, which consists of a hierarchical sequence of names from the most specific to the most general (left to right), separated by dots. For example: www.csuchico.edu.

Download

To transfer files from an online computer out there, to your online computer.

E-mail (Electronic Mail)

Messages (text, graphics, music) sent from one person to another via computer. See Chapter 7.

Error Messages

Error messages may result from a variety of situations, some relating to the operation of the browser, others to the operation of the Internet network. The browser tries to evaluate any problem that is encountered, and present you with information to help you solve, or get around, the problem. A 404 Error means your browser is unable to connect to the URL you requested. The most common error messages result from trying to bring up a page that is not currently available. The server issuing the page may be temporarily shut down, or too busy with other connections to handle your request. You could try the site again at a later time. However, the page may no longer exist, or it may have a new address due to the constantly changing nature of the Internet.

FAQ (Frequently Asked Questions)

A document that lists and answers the most commonly asked questions on a particular subject. FAQs are usually written by people who have become tired of answering the same question over and over. If you want to find out more about a Web site, mailing list or newsgroups, read the FAQ.

Favorites (Internet Explorer)

See Bookmarks.

Flame

A negative response to an e-mail message or newsgroup posting.

FTP (File Transfer Protocol)

A very common method of transferring or downloading files between two networked computers. Many Internet sites have publicly accessible material that can be obtained using FTP, by logging in using the account name "anonymous." Thus, these sites are called anonymous FTP servers. FTP is also used to upload files to Web servers. Macintosh users can use a FTP program called Fetch for these purposes.

Gopher

A second-generation, navigation program that uses menus to display material. Although Gopher use spread rapidly in only a couple of years, it has now been replaced by hypertext read by browsers such as Netscape and Internet Explorer, which are easier to use.

Home

A button on the toolbar which returns you to the home page. You can reset the home page to any Web site you want. See Chapter 1.

Home Page

This is the introductory, or index page, for a Web site that has hypertext links which, when clicked on, will take you to secondary Web pages. See Chapters 1 and 4.

HTML (HyperText Markup Language)

The formatting codes used to create Web pages that can be read by a browser. HTML looks a lot like old-fashioned typesetting code. See Chapter 4.

HTTP

This is a set of rules for exchanging World Wide Web documents between computers that hold the pages, and computers that would like to see the pages. HTTP stands for HyperText Transfer Protocol, and is the basic protocol for the World Wide Web.

Hypertext

A hypertext document is one that includes links (connections) to other documents. In concept, it is similar to including footnotes in a printed document. However, in a hypertext document, you can switch to the connected item by clicking on a hypertext link, usually indicated by a different color from the surrounding text. In the World Wide Web, links can lead to other documents on the same data server, or take you to other servers.

HyperText Link (or Link)

A word, phrase, or image on a Web page which, when clicked upon, links you to another document, which may or may not also be a hypertext document. These links are generally, but not always, designated by a blue underline (or a blue line surrounding an image).

Hypermedia

The combination of hypertext and multimedia in an online document.

Internet (Upper case I)

A super-network that connects many smaller networks together, and allows all the computers to exchange information with each other. To accomplish this, all the computers on the Internet have to use a common set of rules for communication. Those rules are called protocols, and the Internet uses a set of protocols called TCP/IP (Transmission Control Protocol/Internet Protocol). Many people equate the World Wide Web with the Internet. In fact, the Internet is like the highway, and the World Wide Web is like a truck that uses that highway to get from place to place.

internet (Lower case i)

Any time you connect two or more networks together, you have an internet-as in inter-national, or inter-state network.

IRC (Internet Relay Chat)

Similar to a conference call, only using the Internet instead of a telephone. Basically, a huge, multi-user, live chat facility. To communicate with a person, a group, or a site on the Internet in real time, you type your message with your keyboard. When you are finished, you hit return and the words you typed appear on the screen(s) of all the other participants in the "chat" and their typing appears on your screen. There are a number of major IRC servers around the world, which are linked to each other.

ISP (Internet Service Provider)

A company that provides Internet connectivity and services to individuals, businesses and organizations.

Java

A programming language invented by Sun Microsystems, that is specifically designed for writing programs that can be downloaded to an Internet-connected computer, regardless of platform (Mac, PC, UNIX, etc.), and immediately run. Using small Java applications (called "Applets"), Web pages can include functions such as animations, calculators, and other fancy tricks.

Listserv

An e-mail forwarding program which allows many users to communicate on a chosen subject. The mailing list provider has a central address by which messages can be sent, and then distributed to all subscribers to the list. See Chapter 7.

Login

Noun: Your user name (sometimes called "userid") needed to gain access to a computer system. Not a secret name, like your password. Verb: The act of entering into a computer system, e.g. Login to CARL.

Lurking

A person who is just listening to the discussion (either in a mailing list or newsgroup) without saying anything, is lurking. If you are new to the forum, lurk until you get up to speed.

Mailing List

See Listserv.

Mirror Site

Due to the popularity of some Internet sites, mirror sites came into existence. They are an exact replica of another Internet site. If you have trouble getting connected to one site, for example, because of the high amount of traffic, you can usually connect to a mirror site that contains the same information on a different computer, oftentimes located geographically closer to you than the original site.

Modem (MOdulator, DEModulator)

A device that connects your computer to a phone line, which allows the computer to talk to other computers through the phone system. Basically, modems do for computers what a telephone does for humans.

Netiquette

The etiquette on the Internet. The "rules" of etiquette used on the Internet.

Network

Any group of computers set up to communicate with one another. A network can be a small system that's physically connected by cables, or it can connect separate networks together to form larger networks. The Internet, for example, is made up of thousands of individual networks.

Password

Your private code needed to gain access to a secure system.

PICS

An acronym for "Platform for Internet Content Selection," a model for associating labels with content, originally devised to help parents and teachers and filtering software control children's access to the net.

Portal

A gateway, or entrance to the Web. In common usage, it has come to describe a starting point page with a hierarchical, topical directory, a search window, and added features like news headlines, and stock quotes. See Yahoo or Netscape Netcenter for two examples of a Portal Page.

Search Engines

Directories and search engines are two tools that allow you to search for information on the Web. There are a number of specialized search engines and directories available for a variety of purposes. See Chapter 3.

Shareware

Computer software programs you can readily download, for which the author expects to receive some compensation for continued use.

Telnet

When establishing a Telnet connection to another computer, your computer basically becomes a terminal for the other computer, functioning somewhat like an ATM terminal.

Temporary Internet Files (Internet Explorer)

See *Cache*.

Title Bar

The top portion of the browser's window, that has in it the title of the current Web page being displayed.

Upload

To transfer computer files from your computer to another computer. On e-mail, this is called "including an attachment."

URL (Uniform Resource Locator)

Sometimes pronounced "earl," this is the standard way to give the address of any resource on the Web. A URL looks like this: http://www.xyz.edu. See Chapter 1.

Web Page

A document on the World Wide Web. It is written in hypertext, so it can contain text, pictures, movies, sounds, or links to other Web pages.

Web Site

A collection of Web pages on the World Wide Web having to do with a particular topic or organization. http://www.csuchico.edu/Online_Classroom is a Web site.

Definitions on this list were gathered from the following sources on the Internet:

- *Ask Jeeves for Kids Glossary*
  http://www.ajkids.com

- *Brown's Computer Solutions Glossary*
  http://www.browncs.com/wordsfrm.html

- *Glossary of Internet Terms*
  http://www0.delphi.com/navnet/glossary/index.html

- *KnightWeb's Internet Glossary?*
  http://www.knightweb.com/KnightWeb/glossary.html

- *WebInfo: Internet Glossary*
  http://www.rpl.richmond.bc.ca/webinfo/glossary.html

INDEX

Notes:

Notes:

Notes:

Notes:

To order additional copies of this book, or for more
information about other Internet, technology, and
teaching resources, please contact

ERIC Clearinghouse on Reading,
English, and Communication

EDINFO Press

P.O. Box 5953
Bloomington, IN 47403
Phone: (800) 925-7853
Fax: (800) 809-1302